This book belongs to

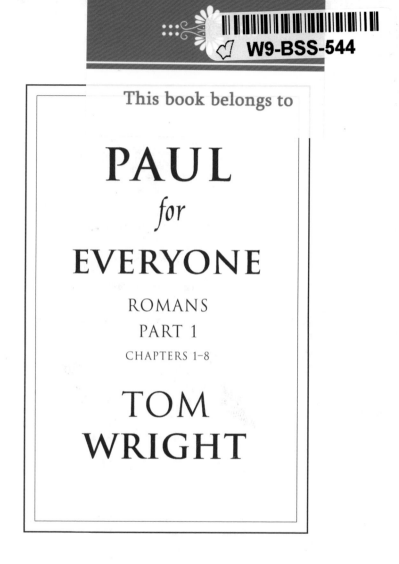

PAUL
for
EVERYONE

ROMANS
PART 1
CHAPTERS 1–8

TOM
WRIGHT

SPCK

Westminster John Knox Press

Copyright © 2004 Nicholas Thomas Wright

First published in 2004 in Great Britain by
Society for Promoting Christian Knowledge
Holy Trinity Church
Marylebone Road
London NW1 4DU

and in the United States of America by
Westminster John Knox Press
100 Witherspoon Street
Louisville, KY 40202

04 05 06 07 08 09 10 11 12 13 — 10 9 8 7 6 5 4 3 2 1

British Library Cataloguing-in-Publication Data
A catalogue record for this book is available from the British Library.

ISBN: 0–281–05312–X (U.K. edition)

United States Library of Congress Cataloging-in-Publication Data is
on file at the Library of Congress, Washington, D.C.

ISBN: 0–664–22799–6 (U.S. edition)

Typeset by Pioneer Associates, Perthshire
Printed in the United States of America by Versa

CONTENTS

CONTENTS

CONTENTS

For
Hattie

'In all these things we are completely victorious
through the one who loved us'

Romans 8.37

INTRODUCTION

On the very first occasion when someone stood up in public to tell people about Jesus, he made it very clear: this message is for *everyone*.

It was a great day – sometimes called the birthday of the church. The great wind of God's spirit had swept through Jesus' followers and filled them with a new joy and a sense of God's presence and power. Their leader, Peter, who only a few weeks before had been crying like a baby because he'd lied and cursed and denied even knowing Jesus, found himself on his feet explaining to a huge crowd that something had happened which had changed the world for ever. What God had done for him, Peter, he was beginning to do for the whole world: new life, forgiveness, new hope and power were opening up like spring flowers after a long winter. A new age had begun in which the living God was going to do new things in the world – beginning then and there with the individuals who were listening to him. 'This promise is for *you*,' he said, 'and for your children, and for everyone who is far away' (Acts 2.39). It wasn't just for the person standing next to you. It was for everyone.

Within a remarkably short time this came true to such an extent that the young movement spread throughout much of the known world. And one way in which the *everyone* promise worked out was through the writings of the early Christian leaders. These short works – mostly letters and stories about Jesus – were widely circulated and eagerly read. They were never intended for either a religious or intellectual elite. From the very beginning they were meant for everyone.

That is as true today as it was then. Of course, it matters

that some people give time and care to the historical evidence, the meaning of the original words (the early Christians wrote in Greek), and the exact and particular force of what different writers were saying about God, Jesus, the world and themselves. This series is based quite closely on that sort of work. But the point of it all is that the message can get out to everyone, especially to people who wouldn't normally read a book with footnotes and Greek words in it. That's the sort of person for whom these books are written. And that's why there's a glossary, in the back, of the key words that you can't really get along without, with a simple description of what they mean. Whenever you see a word in **bold type** in the text, you can go to the back and remind yourself what's going on.

There are of course many translations of the New Testament available today. The one I offer here is designed for the same kind of reader: one who mightn't necessarily understand the more formal, sometimes even ponderous, tones of some of the standard ones. I have tried, naturally, to keep as close to the original as I can. But my main aim has been to be sure that the words can speak not just to some people, but to everyone.

Paul's letter to the Christians in Rome is his masterpiece. It covers many different topics from many different angles, bringing them all together into a fast-moving and compelling line of thought. Reading it sometimes feels like being swept along in a small boat on a swirling, bubbling river. We need to hold on tight if we're going to stay on board. But if we do, the energy and excitement of it all is unbeatable. The reason is obvious: because Romans is all about the God who, as Paul says, unveils his power and grace through the good news about Jesus. And, as Paul insists again and again, this power and grace is available for everyone who believes. So here it is: Romans for everyone!

Tom Wright

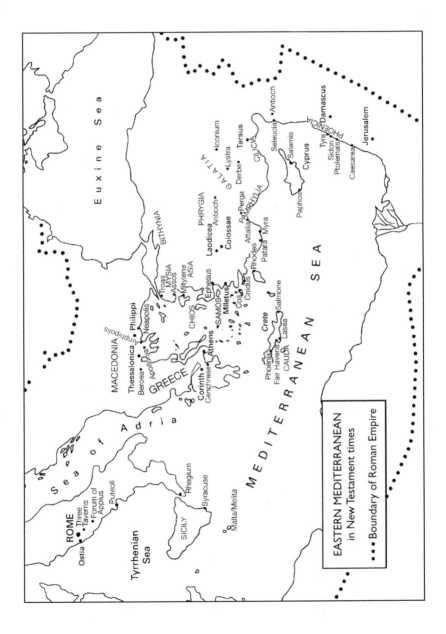

EASTERN MEDITERRANEAN
in New Testament times

• • • Boundary of Roman Empire

ROMANS 1.1–7

Good News about the New King

[1]Paul, a slave of King Jesus, called to be an apostle, set apart for God's good news, [2]which he promised beforehand through his prophets in the sacred writings – [3]the good news about his son, who was descended from David's seed in terms of flesh, [4]and who was marked out powerfully as God's son in terms of the spirit of holiness by the resurrection of the dead: Jesus, the king, our Lord!

[5]Through him we have received grace and apostleship to bring about believing obedience among all the nations for the sake of his name. [6]That includes you, too, who are called by Jesus the king.

[7]This letter comes to all in Rome who love God, all who are called to be his holy people. Grace and peace to you from God our father, and King Jesus, the Lord.

From time to time, scientists have sent space probes to Mars. The object of the exercise is of course to try to find out more about the great planet which, although it's our nearest neighbour, is still over a hundred million miles away. For centuries people have imagined that there might be life on Mars, perhaps intelligent life. There are undoubtedly many new things to be learned, to be discovered. If only we could get there safely and work out what was going on.

A lot of people feel like that about St Paul in general, and Romans in particular. Most people who have at least a nodding acquaintance with the Christian faith are aware that Paul was a striking and important figure in its early days. Many know that Romans is his greatest letter. Some may even have heard of the powerful effect this letter has had, over and over again, in the history of the church: great figures like Augustine, Luther and Karl Barth have studied it and come back with a fresh and challenging word from God. But to many Christians in the Western world Romans remains as much of a mystery as Mars.

'I tried to read it once,' they say, like a scientist describing yet another failed space probe, 'but I got bogged down and I couldn't work it out.'

A different kind of problem lies in wait for those who have learned the Christian faith in one of the great churches in the Western world. Many traditional Roman Catholics, and others in similar traditions, know that the Protestants have made Paul a great hero, and they are therefore suspicious of him. But there are problems for Protestants, too. Ever since the Reformation in the sixteenth century, many churches have taken Paul as their main guide, and have seen Romans as the book above all in which he sets out the basic doctrines they hold. Since part of my own background is firmly in this tradition – which is why I began studying this letter intensively for myself, 30 years ago – I understand the power and importance of this tradition. But I have to report that it has only colonized certain parts of the great planet called Romans. It has mapped and discussed many craters, has analysed many substances found in them, and has laid down well-trodden roads across some of the planet's surface. But there are other parts which have remained a mystery – not least the parts about the coming together of Jews and **Gentiles**, which Paul comes back to again and again throughout the letter. It is time for a fresh probe, for some new mapping, for paths to be hacked through unexplored territory. We still need the old maps and roads, of course. We won't lose anything that they gave us. In fact, we shall find that we get more out of them by seeing and using them within the bigger picture, Paul's own larger picture, of God, Jesus, the world and ourselves.

To understand the first seven verses of the letter, let's stay with the image of space travel, but see Romans not now as a planet but as a rocket. It is designed to take us a very long way, and is kitted out with all kinds of things we shall need as we travel and when we arrive at our far-off destination. A rocket like that needs one thing in particular before it can even start: a first-rate, solid, carefully planned launching pad. You can't just set the rocket up in an open field and hope it will lift off successfully. This opening passage of the letter is the carefully, deliberately constructed launching pad for this particular letter. It is worth looking at each part of it quite closely.

Like most people writing letters in the classical world, Paul begins by saying who he is, and who the letter is intended for. But, as in some of his other letters, he expands this formula almost beyond breaking point by adding more and more information on both sides. His opening greeting could be summarized from verses 1 and 7: Paul, a slave of King Jesus; to all in Rome who love God; grace to you and peace. Why has he expanded this simple greeting into the passage we now have?

He wants to concentrate particularly on the **good news**, or, as many translations put it, 'the **gospel**'. The word 'gospel' doesn't occur very often in the letter, but it lies underneath everything Paul says. Here he lays out what this 'gospel' actually is, partly because this defines who Paul himself is (he has been 'set apart' for the particular job of announcing this gospel) and partly because the gospel itself creates a map on which you can see the whole world, and find where you belong in it. That's what verses 5 and 6 are doing: the gospel claims the whole world for King Jesus, and that includes the Christians in Rome.

But isn't it rather odd to put it like that? Isn't it actually rather daring, perhaps even somewhat risky? Fancy writing like this to Rome of all places, the greatest city of the world at the time, the home of the most powerful man in the world, the Caesar, whose official titles included 'son of god', whose birthday was hailed as 'good news', and who claimed the allegiance, the loyalty, of the greatest empire the world had ever seen! But Paul knows exactly what he is doing. Jesus is the *true* king, the world's rightful Lord, and it is vital that the Christians in Rome itself know this and live by it.

In fact, what Paul says about Jesus in this passage, especially verses 3 and 4, seems almost designed to stake a claim which puts that of Caesar in the shade. Jesus is the true '**son of God**'. He comes from a royal house far older than anything Rome can claim: that of **David**, a thousand years before. His **resurrection**, which Paul sees not as a strange freak or bizarre **miracle** but as the beginning of 'the resurrection of the dead' for which most Jews had been longing, is the sign of a power which trumps that of tyrants and bullies the world over. Death is their final weapon, and he has broken it.

But Paul isn't just writing this with an eye on Caesar. He is drawing on the deep riches of Israel's prophecies and psalms, as he implies in verse 2. There were many different ideas around within first-century Judaism about a king who might come to rule over Israel and rescue the nation from foreign oppression (which in Paul's day meant, ultimately, Rome). Paul, guided by what he knows of Jesus, and especially his cross and resurrection, pulls out one strand in particular, that of the coming king who would be God's son (2 Samuel 7.14; Psalm 2.7; and elsewhere). This is the 'good news': it has happened! God has done it! The king has come!

So how is the king claiming the world as his own? By sending ambassadors out into that world with the good news. These 'ambassadors' are called '**apostles**', which simply means 'sent-out people'. That is the point Paul is making when he refers to his own work in verses 1 and 5.

The 'good news' is not, first and foremost, about something that can happen to us. What happens to us through the 'gospel' is indeed dramatic and exciting: God's good news will catch us up and transform our lives and our hopes like nothing else. But the 'good news' which Paul announces is primarily good news about something that has happened, events through which the world is now a different place. It is about what God has done in Jesus, the **Messiah**, Israel's true king, the world's true Lord.

This means that verses 6 and 7, though originally addressed to people in one ancient city, open up to include us as well. We, too, are called to 'believing obedience' (verse 5). The gospel isn't like an advertisement for a product we might or might not want to buy, depending on how we felt at the time. It is more like a command from an authority we would be foolish to resist. Caesar's messengers didn't go round the world saying 'Caesar is lord, so if you feel you need to have a Roman-empire kind of experience, you might want to submit to him.' The challenge of Paul's gospel is that someone very different to Caesar, exercising a very different kind of power, is the world's true lord. It will take the whole letter, now well and truly launched, to discover what that means in practice.

ROMANS 1.8–13

Paul Longs to See the Roman Christians

[8]Let me say first that I thank my God for all of you, through Jesus the king, because all the world has heard the news of your faith. [9]God is my witness – the God I worship in my spirit, in the good news of his son – that I never stop remembering you [10]in my prayers. I ask God again and again that somehow at last I may now be able, in his good purposes, to come to you. [11]I'm longing to see you! I want to share with you some spiritual blessing to give you strength; [12]that is, I want to encourage you, and be encouraged by you, in the faith we share. [13]I really do want you to know, my dear family, that I've often made plans to come to you; it's just that up to now something has always got in the way. I want to bear some fruit among you, as I have been doing among the other nations.

The first time I went to Rome there was a great deal to see. I knew about many of the classical sites, the spectacular buildings, the ancient palaces, the Forum, and so on. But there were many surprises as well. One in particular which I still find extraordinary is that the middle of the city is liable to serious flooding. The River Tiber runs through it, twisting and turning, and several parts of the town are low-lying and vulnerable. Many buildings near the river have markers which show how high the various floods – and there have been lots of them – have come. Why, I still wonder, did they build in such a dangerous place?

In ancient Rome as today, of course, the rich people lived up in the hills, the famous seven hills on which the city stands. The original imperial palace, where the Emperor Augustus lived at the time when Jesus was born, occupies most of one of them. Nero was emperor when Paul was writing this letter; his spectacular palace is on another hill, the other side of the Forum. But then as now the poorer people lived in the areas around the river; not least, in the area just across the river from the main city centre. And that is where most of the first Roman Christians lived. The chances are that the first time this great letter was read aloud it was in a crowded room in someone's house in the low-lying poorer district, just across the river from the seat of power.

Paul is longing to come and be there with them. As often, the opening of the letter, after the launching-pad itself, is a report of what Paul is praying for when he thinks of them. And the main thing he's doing is thanking God: thanking the maker of **heaven** and earth that there is a community in Rome, under Caesar's nose, who give allegiance to Jesus as Lord, who have been grasped by the vision of a different **kingdom**, a different hope, and who share a different **faith**. That's at the centre of it, as we shall see: faith, the belief and trust in the God who raised Jesus from the dead (4.24, picking up 1.4). You need faith like that to be a Christian in the ancient world, as in the modern; and Paul knows that they have it in abundance.

He knows this partly because several of the Christians who are now in Rome are friends of his. Some are even his relatives, as we discover in the greetings at the end of the letter. Travel was comparatively easy in Paul's world, and people came and went on business, or for family reasons, right around the Mediterranean world. But the letter to Rome is unusual in one particular respect: Paul had not himself founded the church there. According to early memories recorded in the second century, Peter had gone to Rome after his narrow escape from Jerusalem (Acts 12), and had been the first to announce to a surprised capital, probably to the sizeable Jewish community there, that God had at last sent Israel's **Messiah**, and that this man, Jesus of Nazareth, had been raised from the dead to be Lord of the world. So Paul is in a somewhat delicate position in writing to the Roman church. He does not want to imply that they are deficient in some way. On the contrary, he thanks God for them and their faith, and looks forward to being with them so that he can be encouraged by their faith as they, he trusts, will be by his.

We shouldn't imagine, of course, that when we say 'the Roman church' there was already a large church building with hundreds of Christians coming and going around it. Forget St Peter's and the Vatican! Chapter 16 gives us a better picture: a number of houses where Christians could gather for worship, prayer, teaching and the breaking of bread. There were probably not many more than a hundred Christians in all, in a city of at least a million inhabitants. It may have been even less. There was plenty of work for an evangelist still to do. Plenty of fruit still to bear (verse 13).

Quite likely the different houses would be groupings of Christians from different backgrounds. As we shall see, Paul has to address, cautiously, some issues that may have caused tension between them. But there is one factor in particular which we need to note at this stage.

Six or eight years before Paul was writing, there had been trouble among the Jews in Rome. It is possible, even, that this had been caused by the coming of the Christian **gospel** to the Jewish groups in the city. But Claudius, who was emperor at the time, had had enough (to say that the Romans didn't much like the Jews would be putting it mildly), and expelled the Jewish community from the city. When Paul arrived in Corinth, some of his first friends were among those who had left Rome for this reason (Acts 18.2). But with the death of Claudius in AD 54 and the accession of Nero, the Jews were allowed back.

It doesn't take much imagination to think how that might have affected the tiny Christian church. In fact, imagination can be kept on track by things that come up later in Romans itself. The pagan Romans, as I said, didn't care for the Jews. They sneered at them and distrusted them. From the Roman point of view, Christianity was bound to be seen as doubly strange and unwelcome: a kind of Jewish religion that made other Jews angry! So if, as seems likely, the church in Rome in the last years of Claudius' reign was composed entirely of non-Jews ('**Gentiles**' is the word we often use), it would have been easy for them to suppose that the new **message** had, as it were, left the Jewish world behind. God had done a new thing. Israel may have been the place where it all began, but now that had been left behind. All those rules and regulations, the **law** with its taboos, dietary restrictions, special holy days . . . all of it was gone. Christianity was now for the Gentile world. So they might have thought.

And then the Jews came back – including the Jewish Christians. Some of those Jewish Christians were among Paul's closest friends; they would have shared his robust view of how God had fulfilled the Jewish law through the Messiah and also transcended it by including Gentiles on equal terms in his renewed people. But other Jewish Christians will have been deeply suspicious of this: surely God gave the law to Moses? Doesn't that mean that every word of it is valid for all time? Supposing they found themselves living alongside a house-church composed mostly of Gentile Christians who celebrated their freedom from the law, how would they feel? Suspicion, fuelled by the social tensions among Rome's cosmopolitan mix of peoples, might easily turn to hostility.

Paul will address this step by step in the letter. It's important that, all the way through, we hold in our minds a historical picture of the Romans' church and its questions, rather than imagining that it was a church just like one of ours. We shall discover another key point in chapter 15: Paul is hoping that Rome will serve as the base for a new phase of mission, going around the western Mediterranean all the way to Spain. That's part of the reason for wanting the Roman church to understand the gospel he preaches as fully as possible. But at this stage the main thing he wants to do is to tell them he's praying for them. He holds them up day by day before God, thanking God that their faith is firmly in place and praying that he may be able to come and see them and work among them before going on elsewhere. Those of us called to be pastors and teachers in the church should note this carefully. When you hope to visit a person, or a town, the best possible preparation is that you should pray in advance for a chance to see them, and for what God is going to do in their lives.

ROMANS 1.14–17

Good News, Salvation and the Justice of God

[14]I am under obligation to barbarians as well as to Greeks, you see; both to the wise and to the foolish. [15]That's why I'm eager to announce the good news to you, too, in Rome. [16]I'm not ashamed of the good news; it's God's power, bringing salvation to everyone who believes – to the Jew first, and also, equally, to the Greek. [17]This is because God's covenant justice is unveiled in it, from faithfulness to faithfulness. As it says in the Bible, 'the just shall live by faith'.

When I was a boy, one of my regular holiday occupations was making plastic model aeroplanes. I remember the excitement of getting the parts out of the box, carefully cutting them off the stem which held them together, and then looking at the plan to see which ones went where. It was like one of those 'exploded' diagrams car mechanics use, with dotted lines coming out of a picture of the complete model, and with smaller pictures of the individual pieces, including the very tiny ones, at the end of each line.

It was important, too, to know the right order for assembling the whole thing. First the fuselage, then the wings, then the struts . . . and finally it all comes together. Try to stick bits together too soon and you'll end up frustrated, covered in glue, and with only half an aeroplane.

There are several passages in Paul's writings which remind me of that sort of diagram, and this is one of them. The problem, of course, is that we've got it the other way round: here is a complete aeroplane (four verses of Paul's densest writing, packed with exciting and powerful technical terms). First, we have to take it to bits, to see how each part works. Only then can we put it together again and see if it will fly.

Even before that, let's take a preliminary glance at the complete passage to see what job it's doing. Paul is explaining in more detail why he wants to come to Rome. As part of this explanation, he is also spelling out in more detail the effect of the **gospel** he has laid out in verses 1–7. He is coming to Rome as a herald of God's gospel; this is part of his job, because the gospel is for everyone. He doesn't need to be ashamed of it, because it is God's power to save people; and it does this by unveiling God's justice, God's age-old plan to put the world, and human beings, to rights.

But why should Paul say he is 'not ashamed' of the gospel? In today's Western world, people are often ashamed of the Christian gospel. It is so often mocked, sneered at and dismissed in newspapers, and on the radio and TV, that many Christians assume they had better keep their **faith** secret. That, of course, is just what is wanted by the triumphalist secular world around us. But in Paul's day there was a different challenge. As we have already seen, his world was dominated, and the Roman church in particular was to be dominated, by a culture focused on one city and one man. Caesar claimed to rule the world; God's gospel claimed that Jesus did. What was a Christian to do? Practise the faith in private in case it offended someone? Certainly not. Paul may have had in mind a passage like Psalm

119.46: 'I will speak of your decrees before kings, and I shall not be ashamed.' That was what he intended to do. 'At the name of Jesus,' he wrote in another letter, 'every knee shall bow' (Philippians 2.10). That included Caesar.

Paul may, in fact, be gently teasing the pride of Rome. The Greeks, who had ruled the world centuries before the Romans, divided the world into two: Greeks and the rest. They called the rest 'barbarians', probably because their languages sounded like meaningless mumblings compared with the liquid music of Greek. And, for a true Greek, the Romans with their Latin language counted as barbarians. Yes, Paul says in verse 14; and I have an obligation to them as well!

But it is a different division of the world that occupies him for much of this letter. Jews divided the world into two: Jews and the rest. They referred to the rest sometimes as 'the nations', sometimes as '**Gentiles**', and sometimes, as here and in chapter 2, 'the Greeks', because as far as they were concerned the rest of the world was Greek-speaking. (Rome, with its many immigrant populations, had a large number of Greek-speakers, including most of the early Christians.) One of the most explosive things about Paul's gospel, rooted as it was in the Jewish scriptures and traditions, is that it broke through the barrier between Jew and Greek and declared that the saving love and power of the one God was available equally to all. That is central to this little passage, and it remains central throughout the letter.

Now it's time to do our 'exploded' diagram of the key sentences in verses 16 and 17, and see what each bit means and how it all fits together.

We begin with the **good news** as God's power. Paul has already spoken of God's power raising Jesus from the dead, demonstrating that he really was and is God's son (verse 4). Now he speaks of power again, but it's a power which goes on working wherever people like Paul, or anyone today with the same commission, declare that Jesus is Lord. Paul has discovered, through years of actually doing it, that when you announce Jesus as the crucified and risen Lord of the world something *happens*: the new world which was born when Jesus died and rose again comes to fresh **life** in the hearts, minds and lifestyles of the listeners, or at least some of them. This isn't magic, though it must sometimes have felt like that. It is God's power at work, through the faithful announcement of his son.

The result is 'salvation'. This is such a well-known word that we can easily assume we know what it means and then take it for granted. The meaning we normally assume is 'going to **heaven** when we die'. But the New Testament in general, and Paul in particular, have almost nothing to say about that. Yes, of course, they believe that God will rescue all his people from death. Death is a defeated enemy, and its corruption and decay will not have the last word. But this means, not that we'll all end up in a disembodied heaven, but that God will rescue the entire creation from corruption and decay – and that he will give all his people new bodies, like Jesus' risen body, to live gloriously within his new world. That is one of the places the argument of the letter is going, as a glance at chapter 8 will confirm. But this 'salvation', as Paul often makes clear, isn't only in the future, though that's where its full glory will be seen. It makes its way forwards into the present, rescuing people from the state of sin, and rescuing God's people from trouble and persecution. 'Salvation' is a present reality as well as a future hope. Indeed, when this salvation breaks into someone's life it becomes an event in itself to which they can then look back in the past. They were saved; they are being saved; they will be saved.

This salvation is for everyone who believes. The gospel **message** – that the crucified and risen Jesus is Lord of the world – needs to be *believed*. Paul's word for 'believe' and his word for 'faith' are basically the same, and together they are bigger than our words 'believe' and 'faith' usually seem. If someone says 'Is it raining?' and I say 'Well, I believe so', an element of doubt creeps in: do I actually *know* it? Of course, Christian faith means grasping things we can't see or prove. But faith is the opposite of doubt, not just of sight! It means a settled conviction that God has raised Jesus, and that he is indeed Lord of the world (see 4.24 and 10.9). This conviction is the first thing that happens when the gospel message strikes home, in the power of the **spirit**, into a human heart. And with it goes God's promise, which is one of the main themes of the letter, that those who believe the gospel are declared to be 'in the right' *with immediate effect*, in advance of the final day of judgment (see 3.21–31). This is why membership in God's people is available, on exactly equal terms, for 'the Jew first, and also the Greek'.

Verse 17 contains – as we continue the 'exploded' diagram of the passage – the most explosive idea of all. The prophets and psalms had often spoken of God's 'justice': God is the creator of the world, and longs to put the world (as we say) to rights. Their word for justice, and similar ones like 'justify', and their word for 'right', and others like 'righteous', 'righteousness' and so on, came from the same root. Unfortunately, as with 'believe' and 'faith', there isn't an easy way of expressing this in English. Part of the art of reading Romans is learning, when you see one of the words in the group, to hold the others in your mind as well.

God's justice is in fact, at bottom, quite an easy idea to grasp. If God made the world and still rules it, why do bad things happen? Is God going to do anything about it? The biblical answer is, yes, of course God will do what is required to put it right; but then things get complicated. God doesn't do what we expect. He calls out a single family and enters into a loving, binding agreement with them. This agreement, often called a '**covenant**', doesn't mean they are the only people God loves or wants to rescue. Rather, it means that the way God has chosen to bring his rescuing justice to the world, the way he intends to put everything to rights, is by calling this one family, the people of Abraham, to be the bearers of his plan to rescue the rest of the world as well. *God's covenant with Abraham was always intended as the means by which the creator God would rescue the whole world from evil, corruption and death.* God intends to keep to this purpose and this promise, so that he can bring his restorative justice to the whole world. That is, in the end, what 'God's righteousness' or 'God's justice' means. I have translated the word as 'God's covenant justice' here in order to hold all these ideas together. As it's one of the central themes in the letter, it's vital that we get it straight.

When the gospel of Jesus is announced, then, Paul declares that through it we can see at last how God's 'justice', his 'covenant faithfulness', or in older language his 'righteousness', have been unveiled. *This is how God has put the world to rights,* declares the gospel message about Jesus, *and this is how God will put you to rights as well!*

Once again, Paul insists – the fact that he repeats this idea twice in two packed verses shows how important it is – that in order to benefit from the unveiling of God's covenant justice, his faithfulness in Jesus to the promises he made long ago, it is necessary that you yourself have faith. God has been faithful to his purposes and promises; if you want to benefit from this, you must have an answering faithfulness, that 'believing obedience' he spoke of in verse 5. To back this up, Paul quotes a key passage from the prophet Habakkuk (2.4), who was faced with a great catastrophe coming on Israel and had to learn to hold on and trust God, to have faith in his faithfulness. That is the position he now urges on his readers. In Jesus the **Messiah**, God has shown himself faithful to his covenant purposes and promises, and those who believe the good news about Jesus will find that this faithfulness reaches out and embraces them with a salvation which can never be taken away. When we put the passage back together again, it stands before us, at the head of this great letter, as a short summary of some of the most important truths ever heard by human ears.

ROMANS 1.18–23

Humans Reject God and Embrace Corruption

[18]For the anger of God is unveiled from heaven against all the ungodliness and injustice performed by people who use injustice to suppress the truth. [19]What can be known of God, you see, is plain to them, since God has revealed it to them. [20]Ever since the world was made, his invisible power and deity have been seen and known in the things he made. As a result, they have no excuse: [21]they knew God, but didn't honour him as God or thank him. Instead, they learned to think in useless ways, and their unwise heart grew dark. [22]They declared themselves to be wise, but in fact they became foolish. [23]They swapped the glory of the immortal God for the likeness of the image of mortal humans – and of birds, animals and reptiles.

I have just watched a large copper beech tree being felled. It was a difficult and dangerous job for those engaged in it, and I was fascinated to see how they went about their work, with ropes and other climbing equipment as well as chain saws. But I was still more interested to see what only came into view after the great trunk had fallen and was being cut up into sections to be taken away.

The tree had to come down, so we were told, because its roots were rotten. To look at the tree you wouldn't have known there was anything much wrong. If you'd looked closely at the upper branches you might have noticed a few signs of ill health. There was a certain amount of fungus growing around the base, but (so I thought) lots of trees have that, don't they? It was a big tree, about two hundred years old, and most of it looked fine. No, said the experts, that fungus is killing off the root system. Another year or so, and the roots wouldn't hold the tree against a high wind. It might be dangerous. So down it had to come.

I hadn't been completely convinced. I wondered if they were making a fuss about nothing. But then, as the saws did their relentless work, I saw the inside of the trunk. It was about four

15

feet across. The outer two or three inches were solid, good strong wood. But the rest of the trunk was stained a dark, mottled pattern. The rot in the roots had started to spread inside, up to a height of ten or fifteen feet. Before much longer it would have infected the entire tree. What looked to the casual passer-by as a fine, solid old beech would have become a serious accident waiting to happen.

Paul's explanation for why the **gospel**, the unveiling of God's justice and salvation, is urgently required is that the tree is rotten to the core, and might come crashing down at any minute. The tree in question is the human race as it has worked itself into rebellion against its creator at every level. Humans were always designed to be central to God's plan to rule his creation: that's part of what it means to be made 'in God's image' (Genesis 1.26–27). So when humans go wrong, the world as a whole is put out of joint. That Paul has this wider salvation in view is clear from the climax in Romans 8. But for now he concentrates on the central feature of the problem: human rebellion. From verse 18 right through to 2.16, he lays out a charge against the human race in general: humankind is rotten at its heart, and the eventual crash to which this will lead (1.32; 2.5; 2.16) is anticipated in the signs of corruption, disintegration and decay which we can see, so to speak, in the upper branches (1.24–31). Our present passage, verses 18 to 23, rightly begins with the rotting of the roots themselves.

Human beings were made to know, worship, love and serve the creator God. That always was and always will be the way to healthy and fruitful human living. It demands, of course, a certain kind of humility: a willingness to let God be God, to celebrate and honour him as such, and acknowledge his power in and over the world. Paul affirms that human beings have not lost this sense of God's power and deity, but he declares that they have chosen to suppress this truth, instead of honouring God and giving him thanks. It is important to remember this passage, since Paul will refer back to it when he describes in chapter 4 how the **faith** of Abraham, and of Christians, does in fact give God this honour and gratitude, thus revealing itself as the sign of the renewal of human beings. All trees are affected by the disease of the root; but the disease can be cured, and Paul will explain how.

Here he describes graphically how the disease spreads. What begins with humans suppressing the truth about God continues not, as we might suppose, with evil behaviour – that will come later – but with distorted *thinking* and a darkened *heart* (verse 21). This is the sobering truth which many philosophers have tried to ignore: there are healthy ways of thinking and unhealthy ways of thinking. Thought, all by itself, will not necessarily produce the right answers. By itself, human reason can no more be guaranteed to tell us which way to go than a compass in a room full of strong magnets. One of the tragedies of rebellious humankind is the sheer waste of God-given intellectual powers: think of the clever criminal working out cunning, detailed plans to commit the crime and escape undetected, or the clever dictator thinking how to crush opposition, to keep people in the dark as to his real selfish motives, and to stay in power. Fancy using your God-given thinking power for purposes like that.

Along with twisted thinking goes the darkened heart (some translations say 'minds' at the end of verse 21, but Paul uses his regular word for 'heart'). The human heart was seen by many ancient thinkers as the centre of motivation. It ought to be a source of light; but when humans rebel against God, it becomes dark. This is the fungus at the core of the root. The tree can still grow, perhaps for many years; it may deceive onlookers into supposing it is healthy; but it has already contracted a deadly disease.

Humans can deceive themselves, and one another, about this disease. As Paul points out in verse 22, they can claim to be wise while in fact being foolish. This is one of the puzzles of our own day, where in a world of easy global communication we can see what people are thinking in cultures and settings very different

17

from our own. One person thinks the greatest wisdom is for a country to have an enormous stock of nuclear weapons. Another person thinks this the height of folly. One person thinks the wisest thing is for old or infirm people to be helped to commit suicide. Another person thinks this is the very opposite of wisdom. How can we tell?

Paul will answer that question too, but for the moment the important thing is to notice the underlying point, which he repeats in verse 32: it is quite possible for humans to claim that doing one thing is good and wise, and doing the opposite is bad and foolish – and to be exactly wrong. This doesn't mean that all moral standards are relative, that it's simply a matter of cultural preferences. Rather, it's a sign that we do indeed very easily deceive ourselves, especially where our own interests and desires are concerned.

The first sign of the creeping death that spreads upwards from twisted thinking and a darkened heart into the rest of the human life in question is the failure of worship. We are made to worship the living God and to bear his image. Paul, who clearly has Genesis 1 in mind, points out with heavy irony that humans have instead created idols which are at several removes from reality. They represent the image of human beings, who are themselves mortal, subject to decay and death. Not content with that, they also worship images of sub-human species.

It's easy for people today to laugh at ancient idolatry. How funny they were back then, people think. They carved 'gods' out of wood and stone and worshipped them! But of course we do the same. The modern Western world has worshipped many idols, the most obvious being money, sex and power. Paul is not saying that every individual does all of this, but rather that the human race as a whole worships parts of the world rather than God himself. Twisted thinking, a darkened heart, and worship of non-gods: this is the disease, often unseen by the casual bystander, which will bring down the tree and anyone standing in the way.

This takes us back to the first verse of the passage. God's justice stands over against ungodliness and injustice, two terms which sum up what it means for human beings to go wrong. 'Ungodliness' refers to what happens when humans fail to worship, honour and thank the living God. 'Injustice' quickly follows, in the broad sense of human **life** and society getting out of joint, needing to be put to rights. Truth is an early casualty in war; it is also an early casualty when humans rebel against God.

The result is God's anger, or as many translations still have it, 'wrath'. This does not mean that God is malevolent, capricious, liable to lose his temper and lash out wildly. Quite the reverse. As we shall see in chapter 2, God is kind, patient and forbearing. But he cares passionately about his world, and his human creatures; and if there are types of activity which deface, damage and destroy the world and human beings, God will not let them go on for ever. Rape, murder, torture and economic oppression – the list could go on, and indeed will go on later in the chapter: God hates them all. He is angry about them all. Let's be quite clear: *if he were not, he would not be a good God.* He is not in the business of saying that the tree is perfectly all right when in fact it has a fatal disease.

Nor is Paul. There are two mistakes we can make when we think about evil. Either we can imagine the world is completely wicked, so that there are no glimmers of goodness at all. Or we can think that evil isn't really as serious as all that. Our modern Western society has tended to take the second line, despite generations of wickedness on an unparalleled scale. Paul takes us back to a more realistic assessment. The tree is indeed dangerously diseased, and needs radical treatment.

ROMANS 1.24–27

Unclean Desires, Dishonoured Bodies

[24]So God gave them up to uncleanness in the desires of their hearts, with the result that they dishonoured their bodies

among themselves. [25]They swapped God's truth for a lie, and worshipped and served the creature rather than the creator, who is blessed for ever, Amen.

[26]So God gave them up to shameful desires. Even the women, you see, swapped natural sexual practice for unnatural; [27]and the men, too, abandoned natural sexual relations with women, and were inflamed with their lust for one another. Men performed shameless acts with men, and received in themselves the appropriate repayment for their mistaken ways.

Imagine someone who knows nothing of music coming across a violin bow. It would be very puzzling. It has obviously been carefully made, they might think; but what is it *for*? It's too narrow to be a kind of polishing implement; it's too delicate to be for practical jobs around the house or garden. It's even got a little screw to adjust it to make the hair tighter or slacker ... what on earth are you supposed to do with it?

Only when someone produces a violin, picks up the bow and begins to play will the mystery be solved. By itself, you'd never have guessed that the bow was for that kind of work, still less what beautiful sounds it could produce. Equally, you would almost certainly not have guessed, from looking at the violin by itself, how it was to be played. And yet for centuries they have been made for one another. Only when they are together will either of them be complete.

Already I can feel several of my readers becoming edgy. All illustrations are incomplete and inadequate, and this one is no better than most others. Of course males and females are not like bows and violins. Of course there is a sense in which a male can be complete – as Jesus himself was complete! – without a female, and vice versa. Of course the male is more than a bow and the female different from a violin, and vice versa. Yet the illustration catches something of what Paul assumes as he begins to explain how human life has been distorted away from the creator's intention. There is no non-controversial way of getting at this whole topic. We may as well launch in and see what Paul is saying.

Throughout this passage he has in mind one particular biblical passage, namely Genesis 1—3. You might have thought that if he had been going to describe ways in which humans had gone against God's intention he would have done better to begin with something like the Ten Commandments. Well, he returns to them later (notably in 13.8–10). But, as we shall see, there are problems about Israel's **law** which make it less than adequate for his present purposes. He wants to trace the way in which humans have violated, not simply a 'law' given at some point in human history, but the very structure of the created order itself.

Paul assumes that there *is* such a structure; that is, that creation is not random or arbitrary. Taking Genesis 1 as the primary theological statement, he sees humans created in God's image and given charge over the non-human creation. Humans are commanded to be fruitful: they are to celebrate, in their male-plus-female complementarity, the abundant life-generating capacity of God's good world. And they are charged with bringing God's order to the world, acting as stewards of the garden and all that is in it. Males and females are very different, and they are designed to work together to make, with God, the music of creation. Something deep within the structure of the world responds to the coming together of like and unlike, something which cannot be reached by the mere joining together of like and like.

This helps to explain the otherwise baffling fact that the very first instance Paul gives of what he sees as the corruption of human **life** is the practice of homosexual relations. Why on earth, we think, would he single out this particular behaviour and place it at the top of the list? The answer is not simply (as many have suggested) that as a Jew he was particularly disgusted by this behaviour, which many pagan cultures accepted, and indeed celebrated, but which Judaism had always banned. Nor is it merely that the emperor, Nero himself, was known to indulge in homosexual practice, as well as various types of bizarre heterosexual behaviour, and that Paul may have wanted to point the finger at the imperial system and its rotten, immoral core. This may have been a small part of his intention, but it is certainly not his central point.

Nor is it the case, as is sometimes suggested, that in the ancient world homosexual relationships were normally either part of cult prostitution or a matter of older people exploiting younger ones, though both of these were quite common. Homosexual 'marriages' were not unknown, as is shown by the example of Nero himself. Plato offers an extended discussion of the serious and sustained love that can occur between one male and another. The modern world has put various names on this phenomenon ('homosexual'; recently, 'gay'; and its female counterpart, 'lesbian'). These imprecise labels refer to a wide range of emotions and actions which it would be foolish to think only came to light in recent generations.

Paul's point, then, is not simply 'we Jews don't approve of this', or, 'relationships like this are always unequal and exploitative'. His point is, 'this is not what males and females were made for'. Nor is he suggesting that everyone who feels sexually attracted to members of their own sex, or everyone who engages in actual same-sex relations, has got to that point through committing specific acts of idolatry. Nor, again, does he suppose that all those who find themselves in that situation have arrived there by a deliberate choice to give up heterosexual possibilities. Reading the text like that reflects a modern individualism rather than Paul's larger, all-embracing perspective. Rather, he is talking about the human race as a whole. His point is not 'there are some exceptionally wicked people out there who do these revolting things' but 'the fact that such clear distortions of the creator's male-plus-female intention occur in the world indicates that the human race as a whole is guilty of a character-twisting idolatry'. He sees the practice of same-sex relations as a sign that the human world in general is out of joint.

This out-of-jointness, he says, is the result of God allowing people to follow lust wherever it leads – once they have lost their grip on God's truth and, like Adam and Eve in the garden, listened to the voice of the creature rather than the voice of God (this seems to be what he has in mind in verse 25). When, later, he describes Abraham's **faith** and its results (4.18–22) he is deliberately showing how the problems of chapter 1 have been undone through humans trusting God and once more giving him glory. Only when we look at this larger context can we see the deep underlying points Paul is making. Only when we do that can we avoid the shallow readings of this passage that have, unfortunately, made discussion of a complex subject more difficult even than it already is.

Paul repeats 'God gave them up' (verses 24 and 26; it comes again in verse 28). When God gives human beings responsibility he means it. The choices we make, not only individually but as a species, are choices whose consequences God, alarmingly, allows us to explore. He will warn us; he will give us opportunities to **repent** and change course; but if we choose idolatry we must expect our humanness, bit by bit, to dissolve. When you worship the God in whose image you are made, you reflect that image more brightly, and become more fully and truly human. When you (and by 'you' I mean the human race as a whole, not simply individuals) worship something other than the living God, something that is itself merely another created object, and hence subject to decay and death, you diminish that image-bearingness, that essential humanness.

This is not, of course, the last word on the subject of homosexuality. Paul has only written two verses on it at this point, hardly enough for us to deduce more than a little of any fuller position he might have stated. But beyond the polemic and rhetoric that fly to and fro on this topic, we find, here and elsewhere in the New Testament, not a set of arbitrary rules, but a deep theology of what it means to be genuinely human, and a warning about the apparently infinite capacity of human beings for self-deception.

ROMANS 1.28–32

Darkened Mind, Darkened Behaviour

[28]Moreover, just as they did not see fit to hold on to knowledge of God, God gave them up to an unfit mind, so that they would behave inappropriately. [29]They were filled with all kinds of injustice, wickedness, greed and evil; they were full of envy, murder, enmity, deceit and cunning. They became gossips, [30]slanderers, God-haters, arrogant, self-important, boastful, inventors of evil, disobedient to parents, [31]unwise, unfaithful, unfeeling, uncaring. [32]They know that God has rightly decreed that people who do things like that deserve death. But not only do they do them; they give their approval to people who practise them.

Some years ago I attended a prize-giving at a local school. The headmaster made an entertaining speech, in the course of which he read out, without telling us who had written it or when, a long description of how the younger generation was going to the dogs. They didn't respect their elders; they showed no concern for cultural life and traditions; they only cared about pleasure; they were rude and slovenly and ignorant and lazy. Eventually he told us that the passage had been written by someone in the fifth century BC, in Athens.

It is strangely comforting to know that our perceptions of the world getting worse and worse are probably the result of our increasing knowledge rather than other people's increasing wickedness. Throughout recorded human history the world has been full of tears as well as laughter, of human folly and evil as well as wisdom and kindness. And I have to say that when I translated the list of human failings set out in this passage I had a strange sense of recognition. *I know these people*, I thought. *I read about them in the newspaper, and sometimes I meet them in the street.* In fact, *I had an email from someone like that just now.* But that's not the most worrying thing. The really alarming fact is that sometimes I see a person like that not out in the street but when I look in the mirror. The line between good and evil runs, not between 'us' and 'them', but down the middle of each of us. (If we aren't clear on that point, Paul will remind us of it at the start of the next chapter.)

The three middle verses (29, 30 and 31) give us the details, some of them literally gory. We hardly need comment on most of them; they speak for themselves. But, to get the full flavour, try asking yourself: how would you feel if you lived in a village where all the people were like that? Miserable, I should think. You would want to move house. Behaviour such as this is inherently destructive, both of itself (we may have met people who have made one of these characteristics their speciality, and have become a hollow shell, consisting now only of gossip, boasting or whatever) and of those whose lives it touches. There is no joy being with people like that. There is no chance of genuine human community. C. S. Lewis once wrote a description of **hell** as a place where people move further and further apart from each other. Read this list, imagine people who embodied these qualities and nothing else, and you can see why.

But the really striking things about this grisly little paragraph are the beginning and the end. Once again, Paul asserts that 'God gave them up'. This is what human **life** looks like when God says, 'All right, do it your own way.' What happens then is that human *thinking*, not just human behaviour, begins to deconstruct altogether. 'God gave them up', he says, 'to an unfit mind' – corresponding to the fact that they 'did not see fit' to hold on to a true knowledge of God. We still sometimes suppose that bad behaviour comes from a victory of body over mind, but Paul knows better. Evil is what you get when the mind is twisted out of shape and the body goes along for the ride.

That's why the last verse of the chapter is so chilling. People sometimes imagine it's a bit of a let-down. 'They not only do them, but they give their approval to people who practise them.' Surely, we think, doing them is the really bad thing, not passing moral comment?

But we'd be wrong. Imagine you're visiting a prison and meet two men who have committed murder. The first one is penitent.

'I knew it was wrong at the time,' he says, 'but I was so angry I did it anyway. Now I have to live with the fact that I know I did a very wicked thing.'

'You're just a wimp,' says the second. 'We live in a rough old world. Who cares about right and wrong? I did the sensible thing when I killed that stupid old man. He was a waste of space. The world is better off without him. The judge should have given me a medal instead of locking me up.'

Whose world would you rather live in? Is it not much, much worse to live in a world where evil is praised and good is scorned than a world in which, though people do evil, they still know it's wrong?

All this points to the critical statement: they know God's decree, that those who do things like that are, literally, 'worthy of death'. Don't misunderstand. People suppose God's laws are arbitrary. They imagine that God (if such a being exists, they might add) has invented a set of rules to amuse himself, and that he then enjoys the thought of punishing people if they don't keep them. The ultimate in that league was the emperor Caligula, who used to have new laws written in small letters and pinned so high on a wall that nobody could see them. Then he'd punish people for breaking them.

But to imagine that God and his laws are even remotely like that is itself part of the distorted thinking of which so much of the world has been guilty. The 'decrees' of God are not that kind of thing at all. They are built into the fabric of creation itself. Evil behaviour is inherently destructive. It points, like a signpost, towards death. This is obvious in the case of murder

26

and other violence; it should be almost as obvious in the case of gossip and slander, where someone's reputation and life are pulled to pieces, often without any chance of redress. People who are self-important and boastful are effectively pushing themselves into space belonging to others, as though the others shouldn't really exist. And so on. God has made the world in such a way that kindness, gentleness, generosity, humility – love in all its many forms – is life-giving, while evil in its many forms is deadly. The steady process of corruption which Paul chronicles in the repeated 'God gave them up' of verses 24, 26 and 28 is not itself ultimate death. That, as the final condemnation of sin, is spoken of in the next chapter. What we see in Romans 1 is the chilling sight of future death casting its dark shadow forwards into the present. If we recognize even part of the picture, we ought to be all the more eager to see what kind of a solution Paul is going to propose as the letter moves forwards.

ROMANS 2.1–11
God's Coming Judgment Will Be Impartial, the Same for All

[1]So *you* have no excuse – anyone, whoever you are, who sits in judgment! When you judge someone else, you condemn yourself, because you, who are behaving as a judge, are doing the same things. [2]God's judgment, we know, truly falls on those who do such things. [3]But if you judge those who do them and yet do them yourself, do you really suppose that you will escape God's judgment?

[4]Or do you despise the riches of God's kindness, forbearance and patience? Don't you know that God's kindness is meant to bring you to repentance? [5]But by your hard heart, refusing to repent, you are building up a store of anger for yourself on the day of anger, the day when God's just judgment will be unveiled – [6]the God who will 'repay everyone according to their works'.

⁷When people patiently do what is good, and so pursue the quest for glory and honour and immortality, God will give them the life of the age to come. ⁸But when people act out of selfish desire, and do not obey the truth, but instead obey injustice, there will be anger and fury. ⁹There will be trouble and distress for every single person who does what is wicked, the Jew first and also, equally, the Greek – ¹⁰and there will be glory, honour and peace for everyone who does what is good, the Jew first and also, equally, the Greek. ¹¹God, you see, shows no partiality.

'Couldn't we just give him one more chance?'

The young man had been working at the factory for just over a month. He was performing reasonably well, but there was a problem. He had a violent temper, and he would suddenly fly off the handle for little or no reason and throw things at anyone within range.

The foreman had sat him down, looked him in the eye, and spoken to him like an older brother. It won't do, he had said. You have to learn to control yourself. This is a warning. Do it again and I have to report you to the management.

But he did it again. And again. And the foreman, with a heavy heart – he quite liked the lad – had gone to the manager. The manager was angry that a problem like this had gone on for weeks without his knowing. He was all for sacking the young man on the spot. But the foreman pleaded for him. Just one more chance. I'll have another word with him. Let's see if he can pull himself together.

It didn't last. Three days later, someone accidentally knocked into the young man in the canteen, spilling tea down his shirt. He flew into a rage, threw the rest of the scalding liquid into the man's face, and punched him viciously in the stomach. It was a sad moment for the foreman, but he and the manager had no choice. The lad had been given a chance, and he'd used it to make matters worse, not better.

At the heart of Paul's view of God's final judgment, here and later in the letter, lies a picture of God not unlike that of the foreman in the story. God is kind – not 'kindly' in the sense of indulgent, a sleepy old uncle who doesn't care too much what people get up to – but kind in the sense of genuinely caring and understanding, and trying to find the best way forward for every single human being. If this were not so – if, for instance, God was essentially mean, ready to pounce on any and every wrongdoing – we would all have been blown off the planet long ago. But that's not how it is. God is patient. Again and again he gives people the chance to get it together, to turn to him in **repentance** and trust, and to find their lives coming back into shape.

But what if it doesn't have that effect? Then, declares Paul in verses 4 and 5, the people concerned will simply have made themselves all the more fit for the judgment which will eventually fall. The young man in the story had no excuse. He had been given every chance. And he had used the breathing space to make matters worse. So it is, sometimes, with human beings.

This is the chapter, more than anywhere else in his writings, where Paul outlines his picture of the final day of judgment. People sometimes suppose that judgment is an 'Old Testament' idea, whereas in the New Testament you find only mercy. This isn't even a caricature; it's simple fiction. The New Testament does of course highlight the extraordinary, almost unbelievable, love of God revealed in the death of Jesus. Paul will himself celebrate this later in the letter. But if people insist on rejecting God's love – and part of the logic of love is that it can always be rejected – there is nothing else for it. God is committed, precisely as the good and loving creator, to putting the world to rights. That includes human beings. Those who live in the dehumanizing ways described in the previous passages are courting disaster. Those who persist in wickedness, despite having every chance to turn back, are positively asking for it. There is no other alternative.

This picture of judgment will not leave anyone feeling

morally superior. I have on my shelves several volumes of writings roughly contemporary with Paul. Seneca is a good example. He thought deeply about moral and philosophical issues, and held himself aloof from what he regarded as common immorality. Yet his own colleagues sometimes caught him out breaking rules he had laid down for others. He and other philosophers of the classical world reflected, in a puzzled fashion, on this problem: how could it be that you might know what was the right thing to do and yet fail to do it?

The present passage opens with Paul exposing just such a chink in the armour of the elevated pagan moralist. Of course, such a person might say, I quite agree with you in your denunciation of the awful immorality that goes on all around. I am as shocked and appalled as you are. But surely you would agree that people like us are different? That with a little education and willpower we can rise above all that and live the life of virtue to which all truly sensible people aspire?

Not at all, declares Paul in one of his most trenchant moods. You have no excuse – because, even while you sit in judgment on these poor benighted souls you so despise, you are secretly doing the same things yourself! Of course, Paul does not imagine that every single pagan moralist does every single one of the things mentioned in the second half of chapter 1. But the moral law, as a great teacher of mine once put it, is like a sheet of glass. If it is broken, it is broken. All truly wise thinkers, from Socrates downwards, know that they break it again and again.

Neither Greek nor Roman religion or philosophy had any doctrine of a final judgment. But it was central to Judaism, and Paul places it firmly against the ancient pagan world in this passage. There is a God who, as creator, is responsible for the world, and he will put it to rights. And when he does so, he will act with complete impartiality, as accords with strict justice. Paul, as a Christian theologian, does not unsay any of this basic Jewish doctrine. There will indeed be a last judgment, and it will accord with the totality of the life that each person has led.

Sometimes Christians have imagined that Paul's doctrine of '**justification** by **faith**' (see chapters 3 and 4 in particular) means the abolition of a final judgment according to works, but Paul never says that. His theology is more robust than many traditions have given him credit for. He can look the world in the face and speak of the justice of God.

ROMANS 2.12–16

How God's Impartial Judgment Will Work

[12]Everyone who sinned outside the law, you see, will be judged outside the law – and those who sinned from within the law will be judged through the law. [13]After all, it isn't those who *hear* the law who are in the right before God. It's those who *do* the law who will be declared to be in the right!

[14]This is how it works out. Gentiles don't possess the law as their birthright; but whenever they do what the law says, they are a law for themselves, despite not possessing the law. [15]They show that the work of the law is written on their hearts. Their conscience bears witness as well, and their thoughts will run this way and that, sometimes accusing them and sometimes excusing, [16]on the day when (according to the gospel I proclaim) God judges all human secrets through King Jesus.

I mentioned not long ago the mad Emperor Caligula, who had new laws pinned up in places where people couldn't read them. Well, once Paul has declared that God will judge the whole human race with complete impartiality, he has to face a problem of that sort. Surely God's own people, the Jews, have a head start? Hasn't God given them his **law**? Doesn't that mean they have a far better chance of doing what he wants? Isn't that unfair on everybody else?

This question will come back again and again in Romans, each time from a slightly different angle. In the very next passage, for instance, Paul will turn and address the Jew specifically, and will show that, while Jews are indeed privileged in possessing the law, their privilege has done them no good, because, as the prophets pointed out, Israel as a whole has lamentably failed to keep the law.

But in order to get our minds round even these early steps in the argument, we must grasp one thing in particular. When Paul talks about 'the law' he means the Jewish law, the **Torah**, the law given to Moses on Mount Sinai as the way of life for the people redeemed at the **Exodus**. It is, as we might say, Israel-specific. The whole point of the present passage is that **Gentiles**, the non-Jewish nations, don't possess it. People often talk vaguely about 'law' in Paul as though, while it obviously includes the Jewish law, it really means something much larger, a general moral law to which all humans are subject. But that's not how Paul uses the word. As we see very clearly both in this letter and in Galatians, he has in mind a specific historical sequence in which God gave the law to Israel, through Moses, many years after the promise made to Abraham.

A second thing comes to the fore in the present passage which, again, many people find difficult to understand. People who have been taught about Paul, in Sunday school or church, often grasp one central part of his teaching too well, and leave no room for other parts which go with it. I have in mind specifically his teaching about '**justification** by **faith**', which, as we shall see in the next chapter, means that those who believe in Jesus as the risen Lord of the world are declared already, on the basis of that faith, to belong to God's people. They are already marked out as the people whose sins are forgiven. They form the new **covenant** community which God is creating in fulfilment of his ancient promise. Faith, not works! It is a wonderful, liberating, glorious truth.

But people often forget (though Paul makes it crystal clear) that 'justification by faith' is a truth about *the present time*, about how you can tell in the present, in advance of the future judgment, who God's people really are – and therefore how you can know that you, too, belong to that people, that your own sins really have been forgiven. But whenever Paul looks at the *future* day of judgment, which is what our present passage is about, he remains equally clear. The future judgment will take place on the basis of the entire life a person has led. He has already said this in the previous passage (2.7–10). He repeats it in 14.10.

Some people, puzzling over this, have suggested that maybe he is setting it up as a theoretical possibility which he will then show to be, in fact, impossible. They envisage him saying, in effect, 'In theory, God would like to be able to judge people according to how they behave, but since in fact nobody would pass that test he has introduced a different scheme.' That doesn't accord with what Paul says here, or in other passages like 14.10–12, and, in other letters, 2 Corinthians 5.10, Ephesians 6.8 and 2 Timothy 4.1. The contrast between judgment according to works and justification by faith is not between a system God might have liked to operate and a system he has chosen to operate instead. It is the contrast between the future judgment, which will indeed be in accordance with works, and the present anticipation of that verdict, which is simply – I know this sounds strange, but wait for Paul to explain it in the next chapter! – on the basis of faith.

At the moment he is still concentrating on the future judgment, but he introduces a technical term which we shall meet so frequently that we'd better take careful note of it here. In verse 13 he says that those who do the law will be 'declared to be in the right'. I have translated a single Greek word with those six English ones, not because I like making things longer but because the English word which I might well have used has such a long history and is so easily misunderstood.

The word, of course, is 'justified'. It belongs, as the present passage makes clear, in the setting of some kind of lawcourt or judicial process. God, says Paul in verse 16, will judge all human beings, not least the secrets of their hearts, through King Jesus.

(The idea of the **Messiah** as the coming judge was fairly standard in pre-Christian Judaism, on the basis of passages like Psalm 2 and Isaiah 11.) Within the lawcourt setting, 'justify' is what the judge does at the end of the trial: he (it was always a 'he' in the ancient world) declares that one party in the lawsuit is 'in the right'. The case has gone their way. The judge has found in their favour. They have a new status as a result of the court's decision. Just as at a wedding the person taking the service says 'I pronounce that you are husband and wife', and that declaration actually creates a new status, a new reality, so when the judge says 'I find the defendant innocent', or, 'I find the plaintiff in the right', that declaration creates a new state of affairs, in which the vindicated person enjoys a new standing, a new status. He or she is 'in the right'. That is 'justification'.

Now we've got that clear, we can see what this particular passage is saying. Paul, remember, has his eye at the moment simply on the future day of judgment, and on the fact that God will judge impartially. He is facing the question: surely Jews will have an advantage, because they possess the law? His answer is No: God will judge everyone according to where they are, not according to where they are not. Those outside the law (Gentiles, in other words) will be judged that way; those inside (Jews) will be judged by the law they possess. What matters, after all, is doing the law, not just possessing it.

What will happen to Gentiles, then? In answering this in verses 14 and 15, Paul writes something which has long puzzled careful readers. Even after years of studying the question, I often find myself unsure which way to read it. Some people think what he means is 'some Gentiles, by following their consciences, really do keep some of the things the Jewish law was talking about'. That is possible – though Paul would not have thought for a moment that such people could actually live the kind of sinless, holy life which a total keeping of the law would produce. Alternatively, he might be hinting at something quite different, something he returns to later in the chapter (verses

34

26–29) and frequently elsewhere in the letter: that a new category of Gentiles is being created by the **gospel** itself, a category of Gentiles who have God's law written on their hearts by the **holy spirit**, and who are thus coming to know in a new way what the law requires. This, too, is possible – though the idea that Christians will face the judgment day with conflicting thoughts, some accusing them and some excusing them, would then be an odd thing for Paul to say when we compare it with, say, Romans 8.31–39. Either way, verses 14 and 15 are a puzzle.

The main point of the passage, though, is not in doubt, and it is one of great ultimate comfort. The world is not in the hands of blind chance, or of a capricious God who will play favourites and leave everyone feeling the way people do after an unsatisfactory court hearing. True justice – the sort that people long for, plead for, thirst for around the world to this day – true justice will be done, and will be seen and known to be done. God will judge all human secrets through the Messiah, Jesus. That is **good news** for a world in which true justice is still hard to find.

ROMANS 2.17–24

The Claim of the Jew – and Its Problems

[17]But supposing you call yourself 'a Jew'. Supposing you rest your hope in the law. Supposing you celebrate the fact that God is your God, [18]and that you know what he wants, and that by the law's instruction you can make appropriate moral distinctions. [19]Supposing you believe yourself to be a guide to the blind, a light to people in darkness, [20]a teacher of the foolish, an instructor for children – all because, in the law, you possess the outline of knowledge and truth.

[21]Well then: if you're going to teach someone else, aren't you going to teach yourself? If you say people shouldn't steal, do you steal? [22]If you say people shouldn't commit adultery, do you commit adultery? If you loathe idols, do you rob temples? [23]If

you boast in the law, do you dishonour God by breaking the law? ²⁴This is what the Bible says: 'Because of you, God's name is blasphemed among the nations'!

In my country, the police struggle hard to maintain their credibility.

It used to be quite easy. The police force had a great tradition of community service; they were known and respected. They knew when to be gentle and let people off with a warning, and when to crack down and stop seriously criminal or dangerous behaviour. Of course, there were always some who let the tradition down. But in general we used to trust the police. When I first travelled abroad I found it disturbing to discover that people assumed the police were in league with organized crime and would take bribes.

But in the last decade or two things haven't been so straightforward. There have been several well-publicized cases of corruption at high levels, and of officers arresting, charging and managing to convict people they knew were innocent, simply in order to say they'd solved the crime. Worse, there have been persistent accusations of racism in areas where large immigrant populations are still policed by an almost entirely white force. The fact that most officers are not guilty of these failings doesn't make much difference. In some areas, trust has broken down entirely. The police are seen as part of the problem rather than part of the solution.

The Jews never believed themselves called to be the world's police force (the Romans gave themselves that job), but many of them did believe, because of a repeated theme in their scriptures, that they were called to be the light of the world. (See, for instance, Isaiah 42.6, a passage Paul may well have had in mind here.) Many, including Paul himself, would have celebrated the fact that God had chosen Israel and given them his **law** in order to make them a beacon of virtue to the rest of the world. Before his conversion, Paul would have seen this calling of the nation of Israel as the rock on which he could stand firm. He was a Jew; God had called Israel to this position; he was secure.

But Paul had come to see, through his recognition of the crucified Jesus as **Messiah**, that things were not that easy. A Messiah who led the true Israelites to victory over the pagans would have fitted his previous world-view just fine. A Messiah who taught all Israel to obey the **Torah** perfectly would have been wonderful. But a Messiah who died a shameful death, a criminal's punishment – that meant that the world had turned upside down. This was how God had fulfilled his ancient promises: by having his anointed one killed by the pagans! This bizarre and totally unexpected outcome forced Paul to rethink the role of Israel as a whole, and to factor into this new thinking a strand of prophetic thought which up until then, perhaps, he had left to one side.

When he quotes Isaiah 52.5 (echoing, also, Ezekiel 36.20 and 23) in verse 24, he is drawing on the very centre of the prophets' critique of Israel. This critique was so damaging that the same prophets could only see the future in terms of total judgment and reconstitution. Israel had not just made a few mistakes. Israel had failed completely in the task God set her. The only way, now, was for God to send a Messiah who would take upon himself the effect of that failure, and, through him, would establish a new **covenant**. Isaiah 52 goes on, just a few verses later, to introduce the figure of the Suffering Servant who would die for the sins of Israel and the world. Ezekiel 36 goes on to talk of a new covenant in which God will write his law on people's hearts. Paul clearly has both themes in mind.

His charge against his fellow Jews – against his own former self – in this passage is based on his awareness, through the revelation of the **gospel**, that what the prophets said about Israel had come true. Israel had failed; devastation and **exile** was the result. The worst thing about exile, though, was not the geographical displacement, which came to an end when at least some of the Jews returned to their land. The worst thing about exile was that foreigners, pagans, were ruling over God's people. That kind of 'exile' was still going on, as the book of Daniel had predicted (9.24–27, a passage much studied in Paul's day).

The point of Paul's accusations in verses 21, 22 and 23, then, is not that he thinks all Jews commit adultery, or steal, or rob temples (Jews were often accused of temple-robbery because, since they didn't believe in idols, they regarded pagan temples as trivial, unprotected by serious religious sanctions). The point is that if even some Jews are doing these things – and all Jews would know that there were plenty who were guilty as charged – this completely undercut Israel's boast that, *as a nation*, it was still the light of the world, able to reveal God's law and truth to the rest of humankind. The fact of continuing sin within Israel merely confirms the prophets' charge: when the nations look at you, they curse God. The only solution now is for Israel's history to come to its climax in the arrival of a strange Messiah who will take this problem, too, on his shoulders, and establish a new covenant in which people will be transformed from within.

Paul never denies the claim of Israel. Some have supposed that in his description of 'the Jew' in verses 17–20 he was meaning to imply that the law was not after all 'the outline of knowledge and truth', and that Israel had not been called to be a light to the world. That would be quite wrong. Paul's point, here and particularly in the passages that follow, is that Israel was indeed God's chosen people, and that the law was indeed the holy law of the one true God. National Israel had failed in its vocation. Paul will wrestle with that problem, too, in due course. But God has not failed. The passages that now follow will show how God has remained true to his calling despite the failure of the people he called.

ROMANS 2.25–29

The Badge, the Name and the Meaning

²⁵Circumcision, you see, has real value for people who keep the law. If, however, you break the law, your circumcision becomes uncircumcision. ²⁶Meanwhile, if uncircumcised people keep the law's requirements, their uncircumcision will be regarded as circumcision, won't it? ²⁷So people who are by nature uncircumcised, but who fulfil the law, will pass judgment on people like you who possess the letter of the law and circumcision but who break the law.

²⁸The 'Jew' isn't the person who appears to be one, you see. Nor is 'circumcision' what it appears to be, a matter of physical flesh. ²⁹The 'Jew' is the one in secret; and 'circumcision' is in the heart, in the spirit rather than the letter. Such a person gets 'praise', not from humans, but from God.

From time to time one of the big supermarket chains decides to try to pass off its own products as though they were made by one of the regular manufacturers. I remember one store a while ago which sold breakfast cereal with a packet design that, until you got close up and read exactly what it said, would have deceived you into thinking it was the real thing. It happens sometimes with soft drinks, too, and other big sellers.

What counts at that point, for the discerning buyer, is not the price, not the outward look of the thing, but what's inside the packet. Labels can mislead. Sometimes they are designed to do exactly that.

Paul's point in this paragraph is that labels, and even names, can indeed deceive. He goes deeper than simply the deception practised by clever marketing. Sometimes the product itself turns out to be not what it seems.

The 'product', in this case, is the chosen people of God, Israel, here addressed as a singular person, 'you'. The outward label, the badge of Jewish identity for males, is **circumcision**. Paul assumes his readers know this, so he can pass automatically, here and elsewhere, from a discussion of Jewish identity in one sentence to a mention of circumcision in the next.

His point is that the badge of circumcision, and even the name 'Jew' which belongs to the ethnic family of Israel, can deceive. Sometimes what's going on inside the package doesn't match the badge, and the name, on the outside. When that happens, the badge means the opposite of what it says. If a Jew breaks the **law**, his circumcision becomes, in effect, uncircumcision – not that he ceases to be physically circumcised (though some Jews, determined to assimilate into the **Gentile** world, tried to have the marks of circumcision removed), but that his real standing before God is the same as that of an uncircumcised Gentile. This wasn't a new idea. The prophet Jeremiah (9.26) had said exactly the same thing half a millennium earlier.

This point is striking enough (and a lot of Jews in Paul's world would have resisted it), but there is more. The outside/inside reversal works in the other direction as well. Supposing, he says, someone who isn't circumcised (a Gentile, in other words) keeps the law's requirements, what then? Paul boldly draws the conclusion: it is as though they are circumcised. What's more, they will then be in the position, over against the circumcised person who breaks the law, that the Jew in verses 17–20 supposed himself to be in. They can sit in judgment over the lawbreakers.

But who are these Gentiles who 'keep the requirements of the law', and who even 'fulfil the law' despite being uncircumcised? Paul knows perfectly well how odd that last sentence must sound to any well-educated Jew. Circumcision was one of the law's commandments; how then can an uncircumcised person be 'fulfilling the law'? (The same point occurs in 1 Corinthians 7.19, and I suspect that on both occasions Paul intended it to sound darkly funny.)

The answer comes through the biblical echoes in verses 28 and 29. Paul is referring, not to any Gentile who happens to make a special moral effort, but to those who have God's law written on their hearts by the **spirit**. When we check across to other passages where he says more or less the same thing (as he does, for instance, in 2 Corinthians 3.1–6) it is clear that he is talking about Gentiles who have become Christians. In line with the prophecies of Jeremiah 31 and Ezekiel 36, and for that matter with the explosive spiritual experience of all the early Christians, Paul believed that through Jesus the **Messiah** Israel's God had renewed the **covenant**, and was now welcoming into that new family all those, irrespective of ethnic background and hence of outward badges like circumcision, who believed the **gospel**. He is here sketching in, very briefly, the much fuller picture of Christian **life**, of the renewal of the heart by God's spirit, to which he will return in passages like chapters 8 and 12.

This leads him to a very sharp point indeed, which has been as controversial in our own day as it no doubt was when Paul first wrote it. He declares that the label on the package is irrelevant, and that when you find the real thing in a package with a different label you should call the real thing by the right name even if it comes from somewhere else. He takes the holy and wonderful word 'Jew' itself, and declares that when God works by the spirit in a Gentile heart to produce the true fulfilment of the law, that Gentile is to be called 'Jew', even though he or she was not born into a Jewish family. This radical shift in meaning for the ancient name of God's people continues to haunt this letter, as we shall see, right through to one of its most climactic moments, several chapters away as yet.

What is true of the name is true of the badge. The circumcision that matters is the circumcision of the heart, that strange internal operation spoken of originally by Israel's scriptures themselves (Deuteronomy 10.16; 30.6; Jeremiah 4.4). The prophets had spoken (Jeremiah 31.33; 32.39–40; Ezekiel 11.19; 36.26–27) of God's new work in people's hearts; this, it seems, is what Paul has in mind. He is talking, in traditional Jewish language, about the renewal of the covenant, and claiming that it has taken place in and through God's spirit. He has not

mentioned Jesus in this passage, but it is clear that he understands this new covenant to be the direct result of God's action
through his Messiah.

One more note, an interesting indication of the way Paul's
mind worked. Having described 'the Jew' and 'the circumcised
person' in terms not of ethnic background and physical marking
but of the state of the heart, he declares that such a person gets
'praise' not from other human beings but from God. The point
is this. The Hebrew name 'Judah', from which the word 'Jew'
derives, actually means 'praise' (see Genesis 29.35; 49.8).
Despite the fact that Paul is writing in Greek, where the point
doesn't work, he is thinking in Hebrew. If it's 'praise' you want,
he says – if you want the name that says you can lift up your
head and claim your special dignity – then don't look for it
from other human beings, by boasting of your ethnic status as
'Jew'. Get it from God, when God writes his law on your heart
by the spirit.

ROMANS 3.1–8

God's Determined Faithfulness

[1]What advantage, then, does the Jew possess? What, indeed, is
the point of circumcision? [2]A great deal, in every way. To begin
with, the Jews were entrusted with God's oracles. [3]What follows
from that? If some of them were unfaithful to their commission,
does their unfaithfulness nullify God's faithfulness? [4]Certainly
not! Let God be true, even if every human being is false. As the
Bible says,

> So that you may be found in the right in what you say,
> and may win the victory when you come to court.

[5]But if our being in the wrong proves that God is in the right,
what are we going to say? That God is unjust to inflict anger on
people? (I'm reducing things to a human scale!) [6]Certainly not!

How then could God judge the world? [7]But if God's truthfulness grows all the greater and brings him glory in and through my falsehood, why am I still being condemned as a sinner? [8]And why not 'do evil so that good may come' (as some people blasphemously say about us, and as some allege that we say)? People like that, at least, deserve the judgment they get!

I once carried some valuable jewellery half way round the world.

My wife and I were going to New Zealand. Friends of ours in England were wanting to send something – I think it was a necklace – to another part of the family. They didn't want to entrust it to the ordinary mail, so they asked us if we would take it and deliver it for them. This was in the days before the airlines were quite so suspicious about people transporting packages on behalf of others, but even so we were alarmed: what if it got lost on the way? But we knew and liked the people, and agreed. Fortunately the jewellery made the journey with us safe and sound and was delivered at the other end.

Now of course we could have claimed that the jewellery had been lost, and secretly kept it for ourselves or sold it. We would have been under suspicion, but we might have got away with it. The fact that we didn't do that was because we had been trusted, and were eager to be faithful to that trust. One of the ways people describe this sort of transaction is to say that we had been *entrusted* with something. The point about being 'entrusted' is that the thing that's been given to you isn't actually *for* you; it's for the person to whom you are supposed to deliver it.

Once you grasp that principle, this passage, which some have found very difficult, becomes comparatively easy. Paul's point in verse 2 is that the Jewish people – his own people – had been *entrusted* by God with his 'oracles'. (He uses an unusual word here, perhaps to indicate a 'divine message' in general, and perhaps to recognize the fact that, whereas the **Gentiles** were not expecting anything like the Jewish **law**, they were often eager for 'oracles' from some divinity or other.) The Jews were truly called to be the light of the world, to hold in trust God's **message** for his entire creation. And they were supposed to deliver the message, to fulfil the trust, to demonstrate to the world that God was God.

But they had failed. They had kept the message all to themselves, imagining that it was simply a charter of privilege for them as a nation – as though a postman were to regard his bag of mail as a sign of what an important person he was, and therefore to refuse to deliver it. Some, like the Prodigal Son in Jesus' story, had sold the valuable thing entrusted to them, and had spent the money (that's the point Paul makes in 2.21–24). But the point – the only point – in being a messenger is that you deliver the message as instructed. Going around giving yourself airs as 'the messenger' may look impressive for a short while, but when you don't fulfil your commission it begins to look very odd. And Paul's charge against his fellow Jews, against his own self, is exactly in line with the words of Israel's ancient prophets: Israel has been faithless, a useless messenger.

So what is God to do? God's name, according to Isaiah (as quoted by Paul in 2.24), has been maligned, blasphemed, among the nations, instead of being praised. Not only have the nations not received the right message; they have deduced a wrong one, namely that the God of Israel is a bad god, to be vilified and ridiculed. But God will remain faithful to his original intention. Not only is his faithfulness not abolished by Israel's faithlessness (verses 3 and 4), he will continue with the original plan. What he needs, and what he will himself provide, is a faithful Israelite who will at last carry out the commission.

For that, we must wait two more sections. What is the rest of the present one about?

Once Paul had written the end of chapter 2 he was bound to face the question he asks here at the beginning of chapter 3. If God is creating a 'new **covenant**' people who are to be called 'Jew' despite not necessarily being Jewish, and to be referred to as the '**circumcision**' despite many of them not being circumcised, then what indeed is the point of being Jewish, or being circumcised? We might expect the answer, 'None at all'. Indeed, some have thought that it was only residual Jewish national pride which prevented Paul drawing that conclusion. But this is shallow. He continues to believe – his whole understanding of God, the world and the **gospel** is based on the belief – that when God made covenant promises to Abraham, Isaac and Jacob he meant them, and that in Jesus the **Messiah** he has kept them, and that by the **holy spirit** he will keep them fully and finally. Paul has not abandoned the idea of Israel as God's chosen people. He cannot yet explain how it all fits together, but when he returns to the same questions at the start of chapter 9 he will at last be able to set things out on a broader canvas.

His main point, which we have already touched on, is the fact that, though Israel has indeed been faithless to God's commission to be his messenger, God goes on being faithful to his promises. In setting this out in verse 4, he quotes from Psalm 51.6, one of the great psalms of penitence which acknowledge that God is indeed in the right even though humans, including Israel, have sinned drastically.

But the idea of God being in the right, with humans being in the wrong, makes it sound for a moment as though God and humans, or perhaps God and Israel, are simply opposing parties in a lawsuit. (This was the mistake of Job, who imagined that he and God were locked in a legal battle which he, Job, ought to win. It was equally the mistake of Job's comforters, who imagined the same legal battle, and insisted that *God* must win. The point of the book of Job is to say that both are wrong, since God is not ultimately a party in a lawsuit with humans or with Israel. God remains sovereign and transcendent over even those issues which we find most perplexing.) The problem with seeing God and Israel as opposing parties in a lawsuit is then that God, when he judges the world and condemns the wicked, might look as though he is acting as judge in his own case. This cannot be the right way to look at things (verse 6): God must be the judge.

This in turn raises another possible objection. When Israel fails to deliver the message, so that God has to find a new way of showing his faithfulness, that merely makes God's truthfulness stand out all the more brightly, doesn't it? So why should God then be cross with Israel for not doing what was required? Indeed – one of the oldest jibes in the book – why not simply do what is wrong, so that God, in putting it right, can be seen to be all the greater? Clearly, some people had listened with half an ear to Paul's teaching, had heard him talk about free forgiveness and **justification** by **faith**, and had mocked him with the charge that he was saying people might as well do evil so that good may come. Paul has a quick answer for them: in their case at least, judgment will be seen to be just!

These last three verses sometimes sound like mere intellectual banter. Many people, many Christians indeed, don't normally think in this ping-pong style of argument, and get puzzled to find Paul wrestling in this way. But three concluding reflections may be in order.

First, it is important to think things through. We may not always be able to understand God and his ways with the world. But we must not shirk the intellectual challenge that meets us at every point. If we are to love God with our minds as well as with heart, **soul** and strength (Mark 12.30), it is important to follow the arguments through as far as we can – while always having the humility to recognize that we may not be able to see round the corner into the innermost secrets.

Second, Paul needs to face these questions, but, interestingly, is not ready to deal with them properly just yet. When we get to chapter 9 we will find the same set of questions: what's happened to Israel? Has God been true to his promises? Is God in fact unjust? Why does God still condemn people? When we get there, however, we find them set out at more length. Paul can discuss them more fully in the light of what he has said in the intervening chapters. Romans is like a great symphony. The present passage is a little flash of music which looks ahead to a much fuller statement for which the themes that come in between will have prepared the way.

Third, Paul cannot and dare not leave anyone with the impression that being a Jew, a member of God's covenant people, was after all a side issue. There were plenty of people in Rome, not least (we may suspect) some of the Gentile Christians, who would have been quite happy to draw that conclusion, and Paul resists them throughout this letter. Not only would such a conclusion be wrong in principle and damaging to Christian attitudes towards as yet unbelieving Jews. It would cut the ground from under Paul's very gospel. The whole point, as we shall see later on in this chapter, is that in the Messiah, Jesus, God has found the way to be true to his original promises. Jesus, as Israel's representative, has offered the faithful obedience which Israel should have offered but did not. The Messiah is the messenger who finally delivers the message.

ROMANS 3.9–20

Jews as well as Gentiles Are Guilty of Sin

⁹What then? Are we in fact better off? No, certainly not. I have already laid down this charge, you see: Jews as well as Greeks are all under the power of sin. ¹⁰This is what the Bible says:

No one is in the right – nobody at all!
¹¹No one understands, or goes looking for God;
¹²All of them alike have wandered astray,
together they have all become futile;
none of them behaves kindly, no, not one.
¹³Their throat is an open grave,
they use their tongues to deceive,
the poison of vipers is under their lips.
¹⁴Their mouth is full of cursing and bitterness,

¹⁵their feet are quick when there's blood to be shed,
¹⁶disaster and wretchedness are in their paths,
¹⁷and they did not know the way of peace.
¹⁸They have no fear of God before their eyes.

¹⁹Now we know that whatever the law says, it is speaking to those who are 'in the law'. The purpose of this is that every mouth may be stopped, and the whole world may be brought to the bar of God's judgment. ²⁰No mere mortal, you see, can be declared to be in the right before God on the basis of the works of the law. What you get through the law is the knowledge of sin.

Only twice in my life have I been in a court of law. Neither time was pleasant. Once I was up against a gardening contractor who had ruined my garden and then demanded payment. When I refused, he sued. The proceedings were in French (we were in Montreal at the time). I explained my side of the story but, since the contractor spoke fast in a local dialect, I had no idea whether I was answering his points or not. I asked for what he said to be translated, but the judge refused. I lost the case.

The other time was a civic occasion for the inauguration of a new legal officer. We stayed to watch the proceedings and I wished we hadn't. Human folly and misery laid out for all to see isn't a pretty sight. I felt like a voyeur.

In Paul's world, almost everyone would have been much more familiar with lawcourt proceedings than most people are today. Communities were small and tight-knit. Cases would be tried in public. Everyone would want to see what was going on. So when Paul uses a lot of lawcourt language, as he does here, everyone would be able to picture the setting he had in mind. It's important that we learn to do that too.

The picture is clearest in verse 19. First we have the stern voice of 'the **law**'. It addresses the prisoner against whom the charge is being made – in this case, the Jew who is 'in the law' or, as Paul sometimes puts it, 'under the law'. Paul has already demonstrated that all **Gentiles** are guilty before God. Now Israel joins the rest of the world in the dock.

In Paul's world, if you were on trial and had nothing more to say in your defence, you put a hand over your mouth as a sign. Sometimes court officials would strike the prisoner on the mouth to indicate that their mouths 'should be stopped', in other words, that they were obviously guilty and should not be attempting to defend themselves (this happened to Jesus in John 18.22, and to Paul in Acts 23.2). So when Paul says 'that every mouth may be stopped' he is imagining not only that the Jews have joined the Gentiles in the dock but that all of them together are left without any defence. The whole world is accountable to God: all people are obviously guilty, and must now face God as their judge.

This, then, is the main point of the present passage: to finish off the job of rounding up the whole human race before its creator and finding it guilty. Verse 9 picks up from the rapid-fire discussion in the previous section, which Paul may realize has left some of his listeners gasping for breath, and in effect repeats the question of verse 1: are Jews in fact better off than Gentiles? No, he replies; because I have already placed a charge against both groups (more lawcourt language here). Not only are Jews, as well as Gentiles, guilty of sin; worse, they are under its power.

This introduces another major theme of this letter. 'Sin' is not only an act of wrongdoing; it is a power with, we might dare to say, a **life** of its own. Interestingly, though Paul can refer to 'the **satan**' (e.g. 16.20), he often uses 'sin' as a way of talking about evil as an almost personal force at work in the world. This comes out particularly in chapter 7.

For the moment, though, he concentrates on producing a charge against his fellow Jews. He does not now (as he did in 2.21–24) suggest particular sins of which individuals might be guilty. He contents himself with quoting at length from several biblical passages, mostly in the Psalms. These quotations repeat, from various angles, the charge that God's people, just like the pagan nations, have failed to honour him as God or show him proper reverence, and that their lives have consequently failed to reflect his goodness, wisdom and love.

Paul seldom quotes from the Old Testament, though, without having at least half an eye on the wider passage from which the quotations come. A glance at the key passages – Psalms 14, 5, 140, 10, and 36, with Isaiah 59 for good measure – is revealing. In more or less each passage the charge against the wicked is framed within, or followed by, the promise that God will act to rescue those who are helpless before evil, and to make good his **covenant** despite everything. This is the point to which Paul is building up in 3.21 and what follows. Even when issuing a withering biblical indictment of his fellow Jews, he does so in such a way as to hint, for those who know their Bibles, that the solution is close at hand.

To round the matter off, he returns in verse 20 to the question of the law. Still talking about Jews (those 'in the law') he explains that 'works of the law' can never be the basis upon which anyone is declared to be 'in the right' – in technical language, is 'justified'. He has just quoted at length from the Old Testament, and his point here is directly related to that. If 'the Jew' appeals to the covenant status which is marked out by possession of the law, the law itself replies, 'You have broken me.' 'Through the law comes the knowledge of sin,' says Paul. This looks ahead to 5.20 and the whole of chapter 7, where the puzzles about the law, and why God gave it, are sifted through in more detail.

But his main point should not be missed. Anyone who imagines that they can stand before God and appeal to 'works of the law' as a reason for final justification, that is, for a favourable verdict at the last judgment, is barking up the wrong tree. Appealing to the law is like appealing to the policeman who caught you in the act, or to the legal expert who framed the statute you have quite obviously broken. The thing so many

Jews, including Paul himself, had counted on to separate them out from the wicked world ('resting in the law', as in 2.17) was not only no protection against God's judgment; it would actually count on the other side.

ROMANS 3.21–24

The Unveiling of God's Covenant Justice

[21]But now, quite apart from the law (though the law and the prophets bore witness to it), God's covenant justice has been displayed. [22]God's covenant justice comes into operation through the faithfulness of Jesus the Messiah, for the benefit of all who have faith. For there is no distinction: [23]all sinned, and fell short of God's glory – [24]and by God's grace they are freely declared to be in the right, to be members of the covenant, through the redemption which is found in the Messiah, Jesus.

There are many plays and movies which turn, often at the last minute, on a sudden intervention. Someone arrives, perhaps galloping in on horseback into a trial or a wedding or a lynching, bringing news of a reprieve, or a message from a former lover, or whatever. Just when we thought the action was taking its course, something new has happened which changes everything.

That is the mood Paul creates with his dramatic 'But now!' at the beginning of this section – which also begins a whole new section of the letter, running on to the end of chapter 4. Something has happened. The court was in session; all were standing guilty in the dock; what more could be done?

But something *had* to be done. Several Jewish writers roughly contemporary with Paul pondered deeply over the dilemma that faced God when the whole human race turned away from him. God had made the world in the first place; would it turn out to be a gigantic blunder? God had called Israel, and was now faced with the choice of either favouring that one nation even though Israel didn't deserve it, or seeming to go back on the grand promises made to Abraham, Isaac and Jacob, the promises enshrined in the '**covenant**'. In particular, the world was full of wickedness, and God, as the just judge, was bound to do something about it; but there were also, in the world, many people who suffered bitterly at the hands of oppressors, and who cried to God to vindicate them. How was God possibly to meet his apparent obligations on all these fronts?

This is the problem of *the righteousness of God*, or, if you prefer, *the justice of God*, or perhaps *the covenant faithfulness of God*. We are faced with the question Paul alluded to in 1.17 when he said, anticipating the present passage, that the **gospel** unveils God's justice. If it was simply a question of some people behaving well and others behaving badly, that would be easy. If, in particular, Israel had behaved well and the rest of the world badly, that would be straightforward. But the complexity of the problem – and if we lose sight of the complexity we won't understand the details of this whole section – comes from the fact that Israel was given a commission and proved unfaithful. The bearers of the solution to the world's problem turned out to be themselves part of that problem. If God was to be faithful to his promises, and to the whole creation, he would have to deal with all of this together.

The great irony is that the covenant itself, God's binding agreement with Abraham and his family, was designed in the first place to deal with human wickedness and its consequences. The book of Genesis is framed in such a way as to say: God called Abraham (Genesis 12) to undo the problem caused by the sin of Adam (chapter 3) and so to get the original project (chapters 1 and 2) back on track. Here is the particular dilemma in which God appears to be stuck: faced with a world gone wrong, he made a covenant with Israel through which everything would be put right. He must be true to that covenant, otherwise how will he save the world? However, the covenant people themselves have let him down completely, and are revealed as simply part of the world that needs saving. God cannot do what the covenant people expect (rescue them from their plight even though they themselves are guilty) without being accused of partiality, of favouritism on a grand scale. What is God to do?

The problem, therefore, is not just one of God's *justice*. It is about God's *covenant justice*. The word normally translated 'righteousness' at this point carries all these overtones and more besides. It speaks of the way in which God must be, and will be, true to the covenant, and of the way in which this covenant itself was there to put the world, and human beings, to rights. And now, declares Paul, the gospel of Jesus of Nazareth, Israel's **Messiah**, demonstrates how God has solved all these problems at a stroke. The faithful death of the Messiah unveils, before an unready and shocked world, the way in which the one true God has been true to the covenant and has thereby provided the answer to a world gone wrong, and to humans lost in sin and guilt.

Paul opens this famous passage, one of the best known in all his writings, by insisting *both* that this fresh revelation has taken place 'apart from the **law**' *and* that the law and prophets testify to it. This balance is vital. God's new **word** must be 'apart from the law', otherwise only those 'in the law', i.e. Jews, would receive it, and according to verse 20 it wouldn't do them any good anyway. But it must be a word which, in retrospect, can be seen to be fulfilling all that God had promised of old. Paul insists, here and elsewhere, that God does not change his mind. His word does not fail.

What was needed, as we saw at the start of chapter 3, was for God's faithfulness to be put into operation, not by scrapping the covenant plan to save the world through Israel and start again by some different route, but through, somehow, the arrival of a faithful Israelite who would offer God the faithful obedience which Israel should have offered but failed to do. Israel, called to be the messenger of God's saving plan, had corrupted the vocation into mere privilege and had failed to pass the **message** on. Now we see the faithful Israelite Paul had in mind: Israel's representative, the Messiah, Jesus.

The fact that the Messiah *represents* his people, so that what is true of him is true of them and vice versa, is one of the secret springs of all Paul's thinking. We shall find it again many times, but it explains, in our present passage, the notion of Jesus' *faithfulness*. People often translate the relevant words of verse 22 as '**faith** in Jesus', but they mean just as easily 'the faith, or faithfulness, *of* Jesus', and in the light of the whole drift of the chapter we can see that this is correct, and that Paul does not mean 'faith' in the sense of 'what Jesus believed' but 'faithfulness' in the sense of 'the faithfulness of Jesus to the saving purposes God had in mind when calling Israel into covenant'. Paul goes on at once of course, just as in 1.16–17, to stress that those who benefit from this are those who have faith, who believe the gospel. But the decisive action comes when Jesus, as Israel's Messiah, becomes 'obedient unto death, even the death of the cross', as Paul puts it in Philippians 2.8. The 'obedience' of the Messiah becomes, in fact, a major theme in chapter 5, when Paul is summing up where he has got to, looking back especially to the present chapter. 'Faithfulness' and 'obedience' turn out to be two ways of saying much the same thing. 'Faithfulness' highlights Jesus' role in fulfilling Israel's commission; 'obedience' highlights his submission to the father's will.

The result (verse 24) is 'redemption'. This is one of those big technical terms that every Christian has heard but few really grasp. Paul sums up in verse 23 where he has got to in the argument so far: Jew and **Gentile** alike both sinned, and failed to reflect the glory of God which, as his image-bearing creatures, they were called to do. In the classic biblical picture, all together are enslaved, like Israel in Egypt. What God did for Israel then, he does for the whole world now, in Jesus: he provides 'redemption'.

The word is a technical term for buying back a slave from a

slave market, or an object from a pawnshop. But Paul doesn't use it here just as one metaphor, one picture among others. He uses it because, for him, the death of Jesus is indeed the New **Exodus**, the moment when the slaves are freed. He will have a lot more to say about this later, but here he simply states it. God has supplied what the world needs, namely, release from slavery.

This 'redemption' provides what the guilty people in the dock had hardly dared to hope for: not just a pardon, but the verdict 'in the right'! Of course, since they were guilty, this verdict has the effect of a free pardon; but when at the start of verse 24 Paul declares that they are 'freely declared to be in the right' he means not simply that they are 'let off' – which would be remarkable enough in itself – but that they are given the status of being God's covenant people, the people already declared to be 'in the right' in the present, far ahead of the great verdict on the last day.

How can God do such a thing? How can the death even of Jesus the Messiah have this effect? How can God declare that people are 'in the right', here and now, long before the final day when the secrets of all hearts will be disclosed? Paul answers these questions again and again at various points in his writings. But the next two verses, dense though they are, provide his immediate explanation, and to them we now turn.

ROMANS 3.25–26

Jesus' Death Reveals God's Covenant Justice

[25]God put Jesus forth as the place of mercy, through his faithfulness, by means of his blood. He did this to demonstrate his covenant justice through the passing over (in the divine forbearance) of sins committed beforehand. [26]This was to demonstrate his covenant justice in the present time: that is, that he himself is in the right, and that he declares to be in the right everyone who trusts in the faithfulness of Jesus.

Sometimes – and today, as it happens, is one of those times – my desk, and the other tables in the room, are piled so high with papers that I know I will never get them in order by just picking one or two of them up now and then. I have to take a quite different approach, set aside an hour or two, and work systematically through them, answering letters, filing endless papers I may want to see again, and (of course) throwing quite a lot into the waste-paper basket.

The last thing I would recommend is throwing a single syllable of Paul's writing into the waste-paper basket, but with that exception the analogy holds good. There are some passages in his writing which we can take in quite easily. But there are other passages, and this is one of them, which are packed so tight that the only way to deal with them is to sit down and work carefully right through. At some points there will be the equivalent of letters to be answered; that is, there will be, or should be, parts of what he says which should drive all of us to prayer, to reflection, to gratitude and worship. At other points there will be the equivalent of papers to be filed; that is, there will be, or there should be, ideas, images and themes which we will want to take note of for future reference, and place them in a corner of the mind, or perhaps even in a notebook, where we will be able to gain access to them whenever we need to.

This passage suggests that there are at least three main piles into which we need to sort out the material. Very unusually for him, Paul repeats almost exactly the same phrase, which I have translated 'to demonstrate his **covenant** justice'. The first time it is to do with God's dealing with sin. The second time it is to do with God's demonstration that he is himself in the right and his declaration about the new status of his renewed people. And before this pair of demonstrations we find a brief and powerful statement of the sacrificial death of Jesus.

Let's take them in order. Paul has just said that God has provided 'redemption' in Jesus – that is, rescue from slavery. Now he shifts the focus to the language of the **Temple** and of

sacrifice. God 'put Jesus forth', the way a **priest** in the Temple would place the shewbread on the altar (Leviticus 24.8, and elsewhere). Paul combines this with the special word which refers to one item of Temple furniture in particular: the 'mercy seat', the 'place of mercy', where, between the carved angels, God would meet with his people in grace and forgiveness. Instead of the Temple and its symbolism, Paul is saying, Jesus himself is now *the place where*, and also *the means by which*, the God of Israel has met with his people and forgiven their sins. A third idea is dramatically combined with these other two: forgiveness is effected through the *blood* of Jesus. His sacrificial death is at the very heart of God's saving plan.

Paul does not explain further how he understands any of these ideas, or how he sees them coming together in a single image. But together they declare powerfully that the death of Jesus has brought about the reality to which the Temple was an advance signpost. The best way of understanding what Paul is driving at is to imagine, in the back of his mind, the entire picture of the Suffering Servant in Isaiah 53, which includes the idea of the Servant's sacrificial death, and belongs within the larger exposition, just as here, of the way in which the God of Israel has now at last been faithful to his age-old covenant plan ('God's righteousness').

If that enables us to tidy up the stack of ideas in the first sentence of verse 25, what about the second one? God, says Paul, had passed over sins committed beforehand, and was now demonstrating his justice in relation to that act. As he said at the start of chapter 2, God has been kind and forbearing, patient with persistent sinners, giving them a chance to repent.

This might have looked like weakness, or might have given the idea that God did not, after all, care very much about sin. Nothing could be further from the truth. God was obliged, in virtue of being the world's creator and judge, to act decisively with sin – which means, to punish it. Here we discover a further meaning in the idea of the 'place of mercy' in the previous sentence. The same root also refers to a 'propitiatory' sacrifice, that is, one which not only purifies people from sin but also turns away the wrath of God which would otherwise rightly fall on the sinner. Though, again, Paul does not spell out his meaning in any detail, there are all sorts of converging lines of thought which make it highly probable that he sees Jesus in this light as well, as the one upon whom the appropriate anger of God, directed against the sin of the world, has now fallen. (A somewhat fuller statement of the same point is found in 8.3.) At the heart of God's covenant justice, then, is his 'putting forth' of Jesus to take upon himself the anger of God of which Paul spoke in chapter 1. The final judgment day has been brought forward into the middle of history. God's righteous verdict against sinners has been meted out against the faithful Israelite, Israel's representative: the **Messiah**, Jesus.

We may be starting to see some order and meaning in the dense flow of Paul's words. The last idea, that of a verdict being brought forwards into the middle of history, enables us to get hold of the final sequence as well. God's covenant justice, displayed in his dealing with sins through the death of Jesus, is also on display in the free declaration, in the present, that all those who believe the **gospel** are in the right. Once again, the verdict of the last day has come forward into the middle of history. We do not have to wait to discover who will be vindicated, who really belongs to God's people. They already wear a badge which marks them out 'in the present time', as Paul says. Here is the meaning of '**justification** by **faith**': when anyone believes in the gospel, God declares that he or she is truly one of those who will be vindicated in the future.

This declaration carries a *lawcourt* sense: it is like knowing the verdict before the case has even been heard. It also carries a *covenantal* sense: we see in the present who God will declare to be the true children of Abraham (see chapter 4) in the future. And it carries a sense of *the future coming into the present* in Jesus. Those who will find a favourable verdict on the last day (as in chapter 2) are those who are assured of it in advance, simply when they believe.

This demonstrates, too, that God himself is in the right. We recall the puzzle set by writers of Paul's day: granted universal sin, and granted God's promises to Israel, how can God be just, be in the right, be faithful to the covenant, and at the same time do what a just judge ought to do, deal with evil on the one hand and, on the other, rescue helpless people who call to him in distress? What Paul has written here, admittedly in a very dense and tight-packed fashion, amounts to this. In the death of Jesus God has shown himself (1) to be in the right in dealing properly and impartially with sin; (2) to be faithful to the covenant; (3) to have dealt properly with sin; and (4) to be committed to saving those who call out in helpless faith. The last line of the passage, itself very dense, seems to mean this: that, as the faithfulness of Jesus was the means by which God's own covenant faithfulness was revealed, so those who put their own faith in God's act in Jesus are marked out thereby as God's people in the present. God is in the right; we who trust his gospel are in the right; and all because of the death of Jesus. There are many times, in reading Paul, when the right reaction is to kneel down and give God thanks. This is one of those times.

ROMANS 3.27–31

The God of Both Jew and Gentile

[27]So what happens to boasting? It is ruled out! Through what sort of law? The law of works? No: through the law of faith! [28]We calculate, you see, that a person is declared to be in the right on the basis of faith, apart from works of the law. [29]Or does God only belong to Jews? Doesn't he belong to the nations as well? Yes, of course, to the nations as well, [30]since God is one. He will make the declaration 'in the right' over the circumcised on the basis of faith, and over the uncircumcised through faith.

> [31]Do we then abolish the law through faith? Certainly not! Rather, we establish the law.

One of the things that regularly confuses Christians when they cross from Britain to North America, or vice versa, is that, as a friend of mine put it, 'they sing the right hymns to the wrong tunes'. Sometimes there are quite different tunes, not known the other side of the Atlantic, to familiar hymns. Sometimes they sing a well-known tune with quite different words.

Something like that is going on when Paul takes the idea of the **law** – the Jewish law, the **Torah** – and sets it to a different tune. Up until now, he and many other Jews of his day (not only **Pharisees** like him, but other groups too, such as those who wrote the **Dead Sea Scrolls**) would have taken the law and sung it to a tune like this. God gave Israel the Torah, the holy, just and good law. Israel is required to keep Torah; those who do so will be vindicated as God's people when he acts in history to judge the nations and rescue Israel from their clutches. The way to tell, in the present, who will be vindicated in the future, is that they are keeping 'the works of the law' right now. That is their badge in the present, the present sign that they will be vindicated in the future.

This is the doctrine of '**justification** by works of the law'. You can see it set out clearly in one of the Dead Sea Scrolls (the one known, in the labelling which scholars use, as 4QMMT). Often, particular groups would highlight certain 'works' in particular, including their own interpretation of particular biblical commands. They took it for granted that all Jews knew they should keep the written Torah, and they tried to hammer out further laws which, they thought, expressed the Torah even more precisely for their particular circumstances.

This question of 'marking people out in advance', reckoning up in the present who would be vindicated in the future, was always restricted to Jews. They were the only ones who possessed, and hence had a theoretical chance to keep, Torah.

(Proselytes, that is, **Gentile** converts to Judaism, might count as well, but only by effectively becoming Jewish through **circumcision** and taking on the obligations of Torah.) What's more, the question of marking people out in the present, ahead of the future judgment, normally envisaged a restriction *within* Israel itself. The Pharisees (and their successors, the **rabbis**) thought that their interpretations were the only valid ones. There were further splits on this point within the Pharisees themselves. The writers of the Scrolls thought that only their sect would be vindicated, and then only those within the sect who kept the law 'properly'.

Paul's word for all this is 'boasting', and he declares that it is ruled out by the **gospel**. He takes the theme of 'the law', and he sets it to a completely different tune which neither he nor his contemporaries had imagined before. How are you to fulfil the law? How can the law tell you who, in the present, is marked out as among the people whom God will vindicate in the future? It can't – if you are singing 'law' to the tune of 'works'. But it can, if you sing it to the tune called '**faith**'.

This is such a strange idea that many readers, and most English translations, have turned aside from it and translated 'law' in verse 27 as 'system', 'principle', or something like that. That succeeds in making some kind of sense, at the huge cost of making Paul sing a different hymn altogether. Later in the letter, particularly in 10.4–9, he will explain more fully what he means by a fulfilling of the Jewish law through the faith which believes in the gospel of the crucified and risen Jesus. Here he assumes this train of thought, in order to hurry on to his main points. There are three of them, each vital to grasping the nerve centre of Romans.

First, 'justification by faith' itself. As I emphasized in the previous passage, this refers to the fact that, when someone believes in the gospel of Jesus, God declares, in advance of the verdict of the last day, what that verdict is going to be: this person is a member of the **covenant** family, the people whose sins have been forgiven, the true people of Abraham, the people of the **Messiah**.

There are many other things which people have supposed Paul to have meant by 'justification by faith', but this is at the heart of it. It doesn't mean God isn't interested in holiness. It doesn't mean that rules don't matter, that 'anything goes', so long as you have 'a faith' of whatever kind. It doesn't mean that what matters is feelings or emotion rather than belief and behaviour. It certainly doesn't mean that God tried to make people good by giving them moral 'works' to do, and, finding that to be too difficult for them, lowered the bar to make things easier. It means something clearer, more robust, bracing and indeed shocking. It means that when people believe this particular message, that Jesus is Lord and that God raised him from the dead, and trust themselves to the God who has done this, they are assured in the present time that they are part of God's family. This is not because there is anything meritorious in that belief, as though it were after all 'something we do to earn God's favour'. Rather, it is because this faith is the sure and unfailing sign that the gospel has transformed the heart of the person concerned, so that they now truly belong to the new covenant. Faith, as Paul says later in the letter, comes from hearing, and hearing from the proclaimed **word** of the Messiah (10.17).

The second main point is that if this faith is the one and only badge in the present for marking out the new covenant people of God, Jews and **Gentiles** belong equally and on the same footing. This is why 'boasting' is ruled out. If the standard were in any sense 'the law of works', then Jews would have, to say the least, an inside track – as we can see from the Pharisees and the Dead Sea sect. But if a person is reckoned to be in the right on the basis of faith, not works of the law, no such inside track exists. That is why Paul at once goes on to challenge anyone who would dispute his conclusion: are you going to say that God is after all the God only of the Jews? Is he not the one God, the creator of the whole world? Will he not therefore provide a level playing field for the whole new covenant family? Yes, he will, declares Paul. When Jewish people believe the gospel, God will reaffirm them as covenant members on the basis of that faith. And when non-Jews believe the gospel, God will affirm that they have come into the covenant family through exactly the same faith. (This explains the subtle change of wording in verse 30: the circumcised 'on the basis of faith' and the uncircumcised 'through faith'.)

The third point, contained within this last one, is worth drawing out still further. Monotheism is the very centre of Jewish belief, and Paul uses it here to devastating effect against those who would claim a permanent privileged status for Jews. 'Hear, O Israel, **YHWH** our God, YHWH is one'; that was and remains the basic confession of faith, used as a daily prayer by devout Jews from that day to this. This prayer, indeed, was seen from one point of view as the very centre of Torah itself, summing up (in Deuteronomy 6.4–5) so much that had gone before. That, in fact, was how Jesus himself had seen it (Mark 12.29–30). Now Paul goes for the same theme, in order to clinch his argument that 'there is no distinction' (3.22; he reaches more or less exactly the same point in 10.12). If Jesus is the Messiah of Israel, the time has come for all the nations to be invited to equal membership in God's people.

This means that Paul can triumphantly conclude his argument: are we now singing a different hymn altogether? Are we abolishing the law? No, of course not! We are setting it to a far better tune, a tune that in fact God himself has written for it. It was never meant to be fulfilled 'by works' in the way that the Pharisees and others had attempted (see 9.30—10.4). It was always designed to be sung to the tune called 'faith'. Paul is often imagined to have had a negative view of the law, but one of the reasons he writes Romans is to make it clear that that is wrong. The law always was God's law, and it is not abolished. Instead, it is fulfilled in a way nobody ever imagined before: through faith. This is the tune that makes the best sense of the words.

ROMANS 4.1–8

God's Covenant with Abraham

[1]What shall we say, then? Have we found Abraham to be our ancestor in a human, fleshly sense? [2]After all, if Abraham was reckoned 'in the right' on the basis of works, he has grounds to boast – but not in God's presence!

[3]So what does the Bible say? 'Abraham believed God, and it was calculated in his favour, indicating that he was in the right.' [4]Now when someone 'works', the reward they get is not calculated on the basis of generosity, but on the basis of what they are owed. [5]But if someone doesn't 'work', but simply believes in the one who declares the ungodly to be in the right, that person's faith is calculated on the side of covenant justice.

[6]We see the same thing when David speaks of the blessing that comes to someone whom God calculates to be in the right apart from works:

[7]Blessed are those whose lawbreaking is forgiven
and whose sins have been covered over;
[8]Blessed is the man to whom the Lord will not calculate sin.

Imagine a four-year-old boy who has lost his parents in a terrible war. He is old enough to understand, and to grieve, but nothing like old enough to fend for himself. Some distant relatives look after him for a while, but they haven't got room, or the resources, to keep him permanently. They put him up for adoption. He wonders what will become of him, with a mixture of hope and fear.

Then one day a message comes. A couple without children of their own have asked if they can adopt him and bring him up as their own son. His emotions are strongly mixed. Of course, he is delighted. He has a future and the chance of a new life. But at the same time he is worried. What sort of people are they? Where exactly do they live? What sort of life do they have? In short, *what kind of family is he about to join*?

That is the natural question for Paul to ask at this point, granted what he has said in 3.21–31.

However, it hasn't always seemed natural to people reading Romans. Many have read chapter 3 as though it were simply about how individual sinners are justified by grace through **faith**, without reference to God's promises to Israel, to the **covenant**, and to **'justification'** as God's declaration that the believer is now part of the covenant family, the family in and through whom God promised to deal with evil. If you miss all that out, chapter 4 will of course come as a surprise. Why would Paul suddenly want to talk about Abraham?

Various answers have been given. Some suggest that Paul's opponents were keen on Abraham, so that he would want to show he can use him on his side of the argument. Others suggest that Paul simply wants to back up what he's said with a scriptural text, to show that this new doctrine really does 'fulfil the **law**' in the sense of being prophesied in scripture. Others again suggest that Paul is simply giving an example from the Bible of someone who was justified by faith. All of these are ways of not taking seriously Paul's larger world of thought.

So, to return to the point, once we read chapter 3 (and for that matter chapter 2) in the way we have, the question of Abraham is the natural one to raise, just as it was at the equivalent point in Galatians. Abraham was the beginning of the covenant family, the family to which believers now belong. 'Justification' is God's declaration that one has been adopted into the family. But what kind of family is it?

This helps us to understand the question that opens the chapter. It's an odd sentence, and most of the translations get it wrong. There is nothing in the Greek to correspond to what we find in most versions, about Abraham 'gaining' or 'finding' something. As so often, Paul begins with a short question: What then shall we say? And, again as so often, he proposes something which he is then going to argue against: Have we found Abraham to be our ancestor according to the flesh? In other words, is the family, into which we have now been adopted, the ethnic, physical family of Abraham? Or are we related to him in some other way? This introduces the theme of the whole chapter, which is not about Abraham as an example of justification, or as a proof from scripture, or anything so trivial. It is an exposition of God's intention in establishing the covenant with Abraham in the first place, and hence of the nature of Abraham's family. The climax of the chapter comes in a passage often regarded as something of an aside, in verse 17: the point is that Abraham's family is not composed of a single ethnic nation only, but of 'many nations'.

The backbone of the chapter is Paul's exposition of Genesis 15. He quotes 15.6 in verse 3, and then continues to refer back to it, and to the wider themes of the chapter and the surrounding context in Genesis, throughout Romans 4. Genesis 15 is the chapter in which God solemnly establishes the covenant with Abraham, promising him an extraordinary 'family'; that promise was what Abraham 'believed' with the faith that was 'calculated in his favour, indicating that he was in the right'. What follows, in Genesis, is the ceremony which establishes the covenant. This should alert us to something many readers today never even imagine: that for Paul, as for Judaism, 'being in the right' with God is much the same thing as 'being a member of the covenant'. In fact, Genesis 15.6 is tantamount to saying, 'Abraham believed God, and this was the basis of the covenant which was then established.'

The main thing the chapter is arguing against, then, is any suggestion that Christianity might after all be some kind of subset of ethnic Judaism, as defined by 'works of the law'. Abraham didn't come by that route, says Paul, or he would have had something to boast of – which, as Genesis makes it clear, he did not. All Abraham did was to trust the God who declares the ungodly to be in the right. Despite what some Jews in Paul's day were beginning to suggest, Abraham did not have a kind of advance knowledge of the Jewish law to which he gave obedience.

Genesis does *not* say, 'Abraham kept the works of the law, and so God established his covenant with him.' Had it done so, it would have strongly implied that Abraham's true covenant family was to be defined for all time by the performance of those 'works' – which is precisely, of course, what many of the later **rabbis** wanted to believe.

Paul resists any such conclusion. That is the point he is making in verses 4 and 5. He uses the picture of someone doing a job of work, and so simply earning wages as of right. And he contrasts that with someone who does no work, but simply trusts. This, I think, is simply an extension of the metaphor of 'works', a new idea occurring to Paul perhaps at this point. The metaphor doesn't work too well, because in the second part of it Paul talks of 'someone who trusts in the God who declares the ungodly to be in the right', at which point he has forgotten about 'working' or 'not working' and gone back to a straight-forward description of what Abraham in fact did.

But what does Paul mean by saying that Abraham trusted in a God like that, one who declares the ungodly to be in the right? Paul may well have in mind the fact, or at least the tradition, that Abraham had been a typical pagan before he was called by the one true God, and that at the point of his call he was still, in most senses, 'ungodly', unaware of very much about who this God might be or what it might mean to follow him and be conformed to his will and his way. And yet God called him into covenant, a covenant designed to deal with the problem of ungodliness itself and all its consequent human degradation, disintegration and wickedness (1.18–32). Abraham, in other words, started where we all start; in particular, Abraham started where pagans, non-Jews, start. That was where God met him. It wasn't where God left him; God did not say that Abraham was fine as he was; his initial trust in God's promise of a large family was simply the beginning of a process of testing, leading and transformation. Paul refers to that later in the chapter. But his main point is that **Gentiles**, non-Jews, come in, by faith, to covenant membership *exactly as Abraham did himself*. This point will be reinforced from various angles throughout the chapter.

Paul calls a second witness: **David**, the royal author of some at least of the psalms. In Psalm 32, quoted here in verses 7 and 8, the writer begins by celebrating the happiness of people whose sins are not reckoned against them. This is the negative side of the same point. The covenant (we cannot stress this too often) was established to deal with sin. To belong to the covenant, in the sense Paul is expounding it, is to be someone whose sins have been dealt with in the manner described in 3.24–26. To have one's sins forgiven, not reckoned up or calculated against one's name, is precisely what God intended when he called Abraham in the first place. Among the many glorious things about being a Christian, this will always come near the top of the list: that one's sins have been forgiven, covered over, not calculated. David celebrated that a thousand years before the events of Calvary, and Easter placed it for all time on a secure foundation. How much more should we celebrate it today.

ROMANS 4.9–12

Abraham the Father of Both Uncircumcised and Circumcised

⁹So, then, does this blessing come on circumcised people or on uncircumcised? This is the passage we quoted: 'His faith was calculated to Abraham as indicating that he was in the right.' ¹⁰How was it calculated? When he was circumcised or when he was uncircumcised? It wasn't when he was circumcised; it was when he was uncircumcised! ¹¹He received circumcision as a sign and seal of the status of covenant membership, on the basis of faith, which he had when he was still uncircumcised. This was so that he could be the father of all who believe even when uncircumcised, so that the status of covenant membership can be calculated to their account as well. ¹²He is also, of course, the

father of the circumcised who are not merely circumcised but who follow the steps of the faith which Abraham possessed while still uncircumcised.

One of the most solemn moments of a wedding ceremony comes when the bride and groom give or exchange rings. I have taken many weddings in my time. I have also stood there as a proud father for the weddings of two of my own children. Such moments are etched in my memory. The ring declares to the wearer, to the spouse, and to the whole wide world that a new relationship has come into being. A new **covenant** has been made. (Marriage is indeed a 'covenant', a binding agreement between the two parties. The Old Testament prophets sometimes used the image of a marriage covenant, including its stresses and strains, to highlight the nature of **YHWH**'s covenant with Israel.) The ring is a sign and seal of the covenant. It speaks of an endless love, going on and on and on. In my own case, it is many years since I was last able to take my ring off – a further sign, I trust, of the unbreakable bond between my wife and myself.

When God entered into covenant with Abraham, he gave him an equivalent. It was the badge of **circumcision**. Two chapters after the covenant was established, in Genesis 17, God commands Abraham to circumcise himself and the child he has had by the slave-girl Hagar. At the same time, he promises him that he and Sarah, very old though they now are, will have a child of their own. The key verse (17.11) declares that circumcision is to be 'a sign of the covenant' between God and Abraham. So when Paul refers to this very passage, and says that circumcision is 'a sign and seal of Abraham's being in the right, on the basis of **faith**', we are meant to understand that this 'being in the right', this 'righteousness' (to use the old technical term), is essentially the same thing as 'membership in the covenant'. That is why, on this occasion, I have translated it by 'covenant membership'. (I wish there was one English word which did all the jobs that

Paul's single Greek word did for him, but, as I've said before, there isn't. That's part of the joy and the stress of being a thinking Christian: constantly having to figure out the best way of saying essential things in an ever-changing culture.)

The main point of this paragraph is not difficult to spot. Paul has come back again and again to the question of circumcision and uncircumcision, but this is the last time he mentions it in this letter. It was, of course, the big question that lay behind the controversy in Galatia: Jewish Christians were trying to persuade **Gentile** converts that they needed to get circumcised in order to be full members of Abraham's family, and Paul is adamant that they do not. He uses in Romans some of the same arguments as in Galatians, but this particular one is new: he points out, to put it simply, that Genesis 15 comes some time before Genesis 17, so that when God established the covenant, calculating Abraham's faith to his credit in terms of being in the right, Abraham was still uncircumcised, and remained so for some while after that. Therefore, Paul reasons, one cannot possibly suggest that circumcision was a necessary part of belonging to Abraham's family. Had that been so, Abraham himself would not have qualified in those early days.

This leads Paul to the first of the two crucial answers to the question in 4.1. What sort of a family have we come into? Have we found Abraham to be our ancestor in the physical sense – in other words, must Gentile converts get circumcised and regard themselves as members of ethnic Israel? Paul's answer is clearly No. Abraham is the father of all those who believe even when uncircumcised. They too are within the covenant, simply on the basis of their faith (verse 11). At the same time, he is quick to balance this in verse 12. He would not have anyone imagining, least of all in the church in Rome where such things might become inflammatory, that membership in Abraham's family was now for *Gentiles* only! No: he is the father of the circumcised as well. But he adds an important, and abidingly controversial, footnote: Abraham is the father of the circumcised who are not merely circumcised but who also follow the steps of Abraham's faith, the faith he had even before he was circumcised.

Many people resist this conclusion, but it is in fact inescapable. Paul has redefined the family of Abraham in two ways. First, he has opened it up so it contains Gentiles as well as Jews – specifically, Gentiles who believe in the **gospel**. Second, however, he has narrowed it down, so it no longer includes all Jews automatically. Jews – like Paul himself, and all the earliest Christians – are of course welcome, and Paul will argue later in the letter that God wants more and more of them. But the badge they, too, must now wear is that of Christian faith.

Paul must have known how controversial this would have been at the time, and in our own generation it has become so again. We are very much aware of the danger of saying anything that can be construed as even implicitly anti-Jewish, let alone anti-Semitic. And we must insist that this passage, and the rest of Paul, is neither of those things. Paul, in fact, belongs on the same map as other Jewish movement leaders in the two or three centuries before and after the time of Jesus. There seems to have been a sense throughout this period that God was somehow redefining Israel, redrawing boundaries, bringing in a covenant renewal in which nothing could be taken for granted. Paul belongs on this (essentially Jewish) map. Later, he sternly rejects the charge that he might be leaving his fellow Jews out of the equation. But he remains clear: membership in Abraham's family is on the basis of faith. And by 'faith' he clearly means the faith he will describe in detail at the end of the chapter: faith that finds its focus on Jesus and his resurrection as the great, covenant-renewing act of the one true God. All of this will be explored further in chapters 9—11.

The church today, and in every generation, must make sure the door is wide enough open to let in people of every ethnic group, every type of family, every geographical region, every sort of moral (or immoral) background. But it must also make sure that the defining characteristic of the membership for this multi-ethnic family remains firmly stated and adhered to: the faith that Jesus is Lord and that God raised him from the dead. Keeping this balance, and doing so in the right spirit, remains a major task facing Christians in the twenty-first century.

ROMANS 4.13–17

Abraham Is the Father of All Believers

[13]The promise, you see, didn't come to Abraham or to his family through the law – the promise, that is, that he would inherit the world. It came through the covenant justice of faith. [14]For if those who belong to the law are going to inherit, then faith is empty, and the promise has been abolished. [15]For the law stirs up God's anger; but where there is no law, there is no lawbreaking.

[16]That's why it's 'by faith': so that it can be in accordance with grace, and so that the promise can thereby be validated for the entire family – not simply those who are from the law, but those who share the faith of Abraham. He is the father of us all, [17]just as the Bible says, 'I have made you the father of many nations.' This happened in the presence of the God in whom he believed, the God who gives life to the dead and calls into existence things that do not exist.

I had an angry email today from a Jewish Christian who objected strongly to something I had said, very cautiously, about the current problems in the Middle East. (I lived and worked in Jerusalem some years ago, and I still have friends in various parts of the bewildering mixture of ethnic and religious groups.) The main point my correspondent was making was that God gave the land to Israel, and that this promise had been re-affirmed in our own day. Nothing should therefore stand in the way of Israel's security and, by implication, the expansion of its territory to include all the occupied West Bank of the Jordan.

This is obviously a hot topic, and it looks set to continue that way (alas) for some time. But I raise it here because it relates directly to what Paul is doing in verse 13 (to which I directed my correspondent in my reply). The promise to Abraham and his family, Paul says, was that he would inherit – the world! This is breathtaking. Again and again in Genesis the writer declares that God promised Abraham the piece of territory then known as the land of Canaan, roughly the 'holy land' as we know it now. Later writings sometimes expanded this to include everything between the Red Sea and the River Euphrates, far away to the north-east; but Canaan remained the focus. Even when writers much nearer Paul's time expanded the idea of a 'holy land' still further, it was still centred on the original promised territory.

For Paul, however, and indeed for the whole New Testament, the idea of a holy land, in terms of one strip of territory over against all others, has simply vanished. In its place are the beginnings of a completely transformed idea of land: that the whole world – in Romans 8 the entire creation – is claimed by God as 'holy land', and is promised to Abraham and his family as their 'inheritance'. This is one of the most breathtaking revisions of standard Jewish thinking we can imagine. It is certainly as important as the decision not to require **circumcision** from **Gentile** converts. It is of course closely cognate with that dramatic revision of Jewish expectations. The privilege of geography, as of birth, counts for nothing in the new world ruled over by the crucified and risen **Messiah**.

Within the argument of Romans, this revised promise looks ahead, as I just mentioned, to Romans 8 in particular, and, with that, looks wider to one of the main themes of the entire letter. God's **covenant** justice was always designed to put the whole world to rights; certainly, as the world's creator and judge, God is under self-imposed obligation to do just that. So it should come as no surprise that in this chapter, when Paul is explaining how Abraham's family has been transformed into a multi-ethnic entity, he should also insist that God's real intention, in promising Abraham the land of Canaan, was to claim, rule and renew the whole world. The Holy Land was, it seems, a kind of advance metaphor for that larger aim and promise.

The main point of verses 13, 14 and 15 is that if the promises were not made on the basis of circumcision, as we saw in the previous paragraph, nor were they made on the basis of the Jewish **law**. Abraham did not possess the law. It hadn't been given at that stage. But Paul doesn't use this argument here, as he does in Galatians 3. Instead, he warns of something darker. If you introduce the law into the equation, you will end up with nobody inheriting at all.

What does he mean? It will take several more references to the same problem (5.20; 6.14; and then, decisively, 7.1—8.11) before we can put together a complete picture of what Paul is saying about the law. Even then there is more to come, especially in 9.30—10.13. But we can make a start, building on what has gone before in 2.17–29, 3.19–20 and 3.27–31.

The main problem with the law, it seems, is that its function is to show up sin and deal with it – and there is quite a lot of sin to show up and deal with, not least within the covenant people themselves. Thus, if the law were to be a defining characteristic of God's people, God would quite simply not have a 'people' at all. 'Through the law comes the knowledge of sin,' as Paul put it in 3.20; or, as here in verse 15, 'the law stirs up God's anger'. If there is to be a renewed people of God, there must be (in that sense) a law-free zone for them to live and flourish within. Otherwise (verse 14) **faith** – Abraham's faith in particular – would be useless, and the promise God made to him would in effect be abolished.

More particularly, once more, if Gentiles are to come in and belong to God's people on equal terms, there must be space for them to do so, space which is not defined by the Jewish law. The promise must be valid for the *whole* family, not just for one part of it (verse 16). That is why, as Paul says if we translate it literally, 'therefore "by faith", in order that "according to grace"'. This means, as in 3.27–30, that Gentiles can come in on an equal footing with Jews. And all this is to give Abraham the multi-ethnic family God promised him in the first place. The end of verse 16 and the start of verse 17 are the real answer to the question of verse 1. God says 'I have made you the father of many nations' (Genesis 17.5). Paul takes this to mean that the ultimate family promised to Abraham was never meant to be simply from one nation, but drawn from all peoples. He is 'the father of us all'.

How does this come about? Picking up earlier hints, Paul declares that it is all down to the creative power of God himself. God gives life to the dead, and calls things into existence when they did not exist before. Perhaps Paul thinks here of the way in which Jews like himself, in one sense covenant members already, were 'children of wrath like the rest of humankind' (Ephesians 2.3), and needed to be made alive in a new way (compare 11.15); and, on the other hand, of the way in which Gentiles were right outside the covenant altogether (Ephesians 2.12) and were brought in from nowhere. Jewish conversion means '**life** from the dead' (11.15); Gentile conversion means 'fresh creation'. That is how God the creator, the life-giver, has called into being a new family for Abraham, formed of believing Jews and believing Gentiles on equal terms.

Not many Christians, in my experience, make much of the fact of being children of Abraham. We are often content to leave that to Jews, and perhaps Muslims too. Yet the idea of Abraham's multi-ethnic family is important in the New Testament (see, e.g., Matthew 3.8). Is it not time to get this theme out of the cupboard, dust it down and put it to good use once more?

ROMANS 4.18–25

Abraham's Faith – and Ours

[18]Against all hope, but still in hope, Abraham believed that he would become the father of many nations, in line with what had been said to him, 'That's what your family will be like.' [19]He didn't become weak in faith as he considered his own body (which was already as good as dead, since he was about a hundred years old), and the lifelessness of Sarah's womb. [20]He didn't waver in unbelief when faced with God's promise. Instead, he grew strong in faith and gave glory to God, [21]being fully convinced that God had the power to accomplish what he had promised. [22]That is why 'it was calculated to him in terms of covenant justice'.

[23]But it wasn't written for him alone that 'it was calculated to him'. [24]It was written for us as well! It will be calculated to us, too, when we believe in the one who raised our Lord Jesus from the dead, [25]the one who was handed over because of our trespasses and raised because of our justification.

When my family and I emigrated to Canada in the early 1980s, we frequently thought about the early pioneers, arriving in a new and unknown country with no idea what they would find, what the weather would be like, what crops might grow, or whether there was any future or hope at all. We visited pioneer villages with working farms showing how things were done, and marvelled at the sheer guts of the people who had come three or four hundred years before.

In particular, we thought about their first winter. As I write this on a winter's day in England, there is snow on the ground; but the temperature is hovering around the freezing point, no lower, and soon the snow will have melted. It seldom presents a serious problem – though from time to time we have sudden heavy falls, and then we are reminded of what life can be like in other parts of the world. But imagine being in Canada, without central heating, hot water or motorized transport. Your family gets sick; some of your animals are dying; the crops you sowed are buried under several feet of snow, and the ground below that is frozen to a depth of several more feet. February turns to March, and the snow and ice are still there. Just how long is winter going to be? How easy it would have been to wish one had never come, to stop believing and hoping.

And yet they hoped, and worked, and built families, communities, a country. And I am reminded of them – it's not a perfect illustration, but it's a start – as I think of the ridiculous **faith** and hope of Abraham, the faith and hope that started the **covenant** family in the first place. Everybody in his world, like everybody in ours, knew perfectly well that if a couple were childless beyond the age of fifty, let alone approaching a hundred, they were likely to remain that way. And it was then, to them, that the living God, the world's creator, made the extraordinary promise: you will have children as numerous as the stars in the sky, or the sand on the seashore. That is the promise referred to in verse 18, when God says (Genesis 15.5), 'that's what your family will be like'. That is the promise which Abraham believed when it says, in the next verse in Genesis, 'and it was calculated in his favour, in terms of his being in the right,' or if you like, 'it was calculated to him as the basis of his covenant membership'. (The older language, 'it was reckoned to him as righteousness', gives off so many different messages now that it's hard for us, hearing it, to think the thoughts Paul had in his head.) This was the faith at the heart of the family. Faith in the God who promised apparently impossible things and then accomplished them. The phrase 'hoping against hope', which we use sometimes to indicate that we're clinging on even though it all seems hopeless, comes originally from verse 18.

Paul's description of Abraham's faith, though, goes deeper than simply an account of heroic trust in the face of overwhelming odds. It is a deliberate reversal of his description of the degeneration of the human race in chapter 1. It's worth looking back to 1.20 and the verses that follow. What Paul is

77

saying is that in Abraham's faith, and in faith of the same kind (which, as he will show at the end of the chapter, basically means Christian faith), human beings are put back together again and enabled to rediscover what a genuinely human life is like.

This is how it works. Humans ignored God, the creator (1.20, 25); Abraham believed in God as creator and life-giver (4.17). Humans knew about God's power, but didn't worship him as God (1.20); Abraham recognized God's power, and trusted him to use it (4.21). Human beings did not give God the glory he was due (1.21); Abraham gave God the glory (4.20). Human beings dishonoured their own bodies by worshipping beings that were not divine (1.24); Abraham, through worshipping the God who gives new **life**, found that his own body regained its power even though he was long past the age for fathering children.

The result in each case is telling. Humans dishonour their bodies by females and males turning away from one another into same-sex relationships (1.26–27); Abraham and Sarah, through their trust in God's promises, are given power to conceive a child (4.19). Deep within the heart of God's covenant promise lies the fulfilment of the basic command back in Genesis 1, the command which goes with the creation of male and female in God's image: Be fruitful and multiply. As Romans 4 comes towards its end, we realize that Paul is saying, on a large scale, that the ancient Jewish dream has been fulfilled. God called Abraham to undo the sin of the human race, and this is how it has happened. God is the God of new hope, of new fruitfulness, because he is the God of new starts, of fresh creation.

But this hasn't happened, of course, through Abraham alone. He was a signpost, pointing forwards: the beginning of the long, winding road, not the goal. The goal itself has been reached in Jesus, and in the events of his death and **resurrection**. Paul has, so far, mentioned these only very briefly, in the opening formula (1.3–4) and the tight-packed description of Jesus' saving death (3.24–25). But he assumes that his readers will know what he's talking about, and as he rounds off his account of Abraham's faith he brings the discussion right up to date.

He has already described how God will reckon, with immediate effect, that those who believe in Jesus are members of the covenant family, assured that their sins are forgiven (3.21–31). Now he grounds this in the terms of the original covenant itself. Abraham believed that God would give life where there was none. Christians believe that God raised Jesus from the dead. In neither case can this be a cunning calculation, a reasoned position which avoids looking the creator God in the face and trusting him against all the odds. In both cases it can only be a recognition that God is God, that our life and the life of the world are in his hand, that he has already begun his new creation and invites us to trust him to carry it through to the end.

The last verse of the chapter anticipates something Paul is going to do throughout chapters 5—8. He rounds off every stage of the argument in this long section with a reference to Jesus. This isn't a mere pious gesture, smuggling in a mention of Jesus in case we thought he'd forgotten about him. It shows, rather, what the whole argument is all about. It brings us back home to the source and power of Paul's thought. In this case, it draws together what has been underneath the whole of the previous four chapters. Jesus was handed over because of our trespasses; in other words, the massive human evil which has disfigured the world came together and, in the cross, was dealt with as it deserved, in judicial condemnation (3.25; 8.3). He was raised because of our **justification**, our being declared 'in the right', our being affirmed as members of the covenant; in other words, when Jesus was raised from the dead God was not only saying 'he really was and is my son' (1.4), but also 'all those who believe in him really are my people'.

Underneath Paul's neat formula is another reference to the Suffering Servant in Isaiah 53, the one who will 'make many righteous, and bear their iniquities' (53.11). The first great section of Romans ends with Paul saying, in effect: the prophetic promises have come true; Abraham's faith is at last vindicated; the law has been fulfilled; human idolatry, sin and death have been decisively challenged; God has sent his own son as the **Messiah**, Israel's faithful representative, to do for Israel and the world what they could not do for themselves; those who believe in the **gospel**, in God's **good news** about his son, are assured that they are the people of the new covenant, the single world-wide family promised to Abraham.

This raises all sorts of questions, which Paul will now begin to address in the next great section of the letter. But it ought to raise questions for us as well. Do we share Abraham's faith? Do we look in love, gratitude and trust to the creator God who promises impossible things and brings them to pass? Have we learned to celebrate this God, and to live as one family with all those who share this faith and hope?

ROMANS 5.1–5

Peace and Hope

[1]The result is this: since we have been declared 'in the right' on the basis of faith, we have peace with God through our Lord Jesus the Messiah. [2]Through him we have been allowed to approach, by faith, into this grace in which we stand; and we celebrate the hope of the glory of God.

[3]That's not all. We also celebrate in our sufferings, because we know that suffering produces patience, [4]patience produces a well-formed character, and a character like that produces hope. [5]Hope, in its turn, does not make us ashamed, because the love of God has been poured out in our hearts through the holy spirit who has been given to us.

I recently heard of a famous comedian who had been a familiar figure on radio and television for many years. His quick wit and endless supply of jokes guaranteed him a big audience. But when he died, the published obituaries told a darker story as well. He had fallen out with his father when he was still a young man, and the quarrel had never been made up. Then the tragic pattern had repeated itself. One of his own sons had fallen out with him, and had been cut off.

Coming as I do from a happy and supportive family I struggle to imagine what that must be like. Imagine knowing that there is someone there, only a telephone call away, who is one of your closest blood relations ... and yet he won't speak to you, and you don't want to speak to him, or to see him, or to have any-thing to do with him. And imagine that going on for years and years. There is something deeply disturbing about the whole picture – and yet I know that not only the man in question, but a great many people, live exactly like that in relation to someone close to them with whom they have fallen out.

There is an even greater tragedy. A vast number of human beings live exactly like that in relation to God. I listened on the radio just now to a cheerful woman talking about how she was fascinated by religion, how she'd had a religious phase as a child ('I suppose most of us do,' she said patronizingly), and yet how there wasn't a shred of evidence for God. I wanted to ask her 'Which God are you talking about?', but of course you don't get the chance to do that. But I came back to Romans and I reflected: here, at the centre of it all, is Paul talking about a reconciliation to end all reconciliations. 'Since we have been declared to be in the right, we have' – what? a warm glow in the heart? a sigh of relief that our sins have been forgiven? a new understanding of what it means to belong to God's people? Yes, all of those and more, but at the centre of it all we have *peace with God*. Having laid the foundation in chapters 1 to 4, Paul is beginning to build the structure: a picture of Christian life in which all the ancient promises of God are coming true. And at the centre of these promises is the establishment of a loving, welcoming personal relationship between individual humans and the creator God himself.

This seems, of course, nonsense to many people today. The

same radio programme had someone saying how ridiculous it was to think that, if there is a God, he might actually be concerned with every single one of his human creatures at every single moment: 'All those millions and millions of people out there,' she said, 'and here he is watching me tie up my shoelace!' Put like that, of course, it seems absurd; and yet the absurdity lies in the attempt to picture God as just like us only a bit bigger and more all-seeing. The God of the Bible is more mysterious by a long way. He is the creator of the world, transcendent over and above his creation, and yet, because his very nature is love, it is (as we might say) completely natural for him to establish personal, one-to-one relations with every single one of us.

Natural for him, maybe; it certainly doesn't seem natural for us. The reasons for this are obvious once we have grappled with Romans 1.18–32. Not only our behaviour, but our thinking and feeling, have been so warped by rebellion and idolatry that we assume it's hard to establish a relationship with God, and that even if we succeed it will be difficult and awkward to maintain it, or maybe even intrusive and frightening. Well, there are problems, of course. Prayer itself is not easy; Paul will talk, towards the end of the present section of the letter (8.26–27), of a sense of 'groaning' in the **spirit**, not knowing what's going on. But we shouldn't mistake this for a structural problem in the relationship itself.

When we are reconciled to the God who is our father, we discover that he wants not simply to enjoy this one-to-one relationship, but to enlist us in his service in working for his **kingdom**. And that will bring all kinds of pressures and problems which will require us to hang on in **faith** and hope even when we don't sense his presence, even when it doesn't 'feel' as though there's anything happening. We mustn't imagine that our *feeling* of being close to God is a true index of the reality. Emotions often deceive. Paul is summoning us to understand the reality, the solid rock beneath the shifting sands of feeling.

The first two verses of chapter 5, then, celebrate our access into the very presence of God himself. We have 'the right to approach': this is the language of the **Temple**, where certain people get to come near to where God is. 'Grace' here is almost a shorthand for the presence and power of God himself. As a result of being justified by faith, we are, in the old phrase, 'in a state of grace', a status, a position where we are surrounded by God's love and generosity, invited to breathe it in as our native air. As we do so, we realize that this is what we were made for; that this is what truly human existence ought to be like; and that it is the beginning of something so big, so massive, so unimaginably beautiful and powerful, that we almost burst as we think of it. When we stand there in God's own presence, not trembling but deeply grateful, and begin to inhale his goodness, his wisdom, his power and his joy, we sense that we are being invited to go all the way, to become the true reflections-of-God, the true image-bearers, that we were made to be. Paul puts it like this: 'we celebrate the hope of the glory of God'. This is the glory that was lost through idolatry and sin (3.23). When we finally inherit this glory, the whole creation will be set free from corruption and share our new-found freedom, the freedom to be our true selves at last (8.21).

No wonder Paul can then go on to speak of celebration even in the midst of sufferings, the necessary path through which we travel as we share the father's work in this still-corrupt world. Note, he doesn't say that we celebrate our sufferings (in the same way that we celebrate our hope, in verse 2). We celebrate, he says, *in* our sufferings. He sees a steady progression in which God uses our sufferings for the same purpose as he gives us his own presence and love: to transform us into the truly human people we were made to be. That progression leads from patience to character, and from character to hope. We live in a world that wants everything immediately; that has no stability of character except a hollow media image; that wanders this way and that because it has no idea where it might be going.

The **gospel** of Jesus the **Messiah** calls us to swim against the tide on all counts.

As we do so, it gives us something else too. Why does Paul say that hope 'does not make us ashamed'? Why might it have done so, anyway? I think the answer is that the Christian, like Abraham, is called again and again to 'hope against hope' (4.18). We look foolish in the world's eyes, waiting for something we can't see (8.25). But we don't appear foolish to ourselves, because we are sustained by something far deeper, something which grows directly out of the gift of 'peace with God', out of the reconciliation which Paul describes a few verses later. Israel was commanded to 'love YHWH your God with all your heart'. Paul, conscious that the new family he has described is the true family of Abraham, now declares that, through the gift of the **holy spirit**, this becomes a reality for us.

Many translations, and many writers about Paul, understand verse 5 differently. They think it means that God's love for us is given in a new way through the holy spirit. That is no doubt true, and Paul will say something like that in the next passage; but I don't think it is the truth he wants to highlight at this particular point. What he is doing, throughout the section which begins here, is establishing those who belong to Jesus as the true **covenant** family, those in whom all the promises (and all the commands) given to Israel have come true. He has already referred to Israel's central command and prayer, the 'Shema' (3.29–30). 'Hear and obey, O Israel: YHWH our God, YHWH is one.' Now he shows how those grasped by the gospel are marked out as the people who offer this God 'the obedience of faith' (1.5), loving him from the heart.

These verses are packed full with wonderful material. We could go on examining them a lot longer. But the last thing we must say is this: they introduce the long section of chapters 5—8, and in doing so they point out several themes we shall explore in due course. One of the central challenges of reading Romans is to hold the whole argument in your head, seeing how it grows and develops. Paul is not writing simply a few short essays about different aspects of Christian truth. Learn to follow the sweep of thought, and it will leave you breathless at the power of God's truth.

And, of course, at the depth of God's love. Pause for a moment and celebrate, in grateful prayer, the glorious fact of being welcomed into God's presence, at peace and in hope.

ROMANS 5.6–11

Jesus' Death Reveals God's Love and Guarantees Final Salvation

[6]This is all based on what the Messiah did: while we were still weak, at that very moment he died on behalf of the ungodly. [7]It's a rare thing to find someone who will die on behalf of an upright person – though someone might, I suppose, die for a good person. [8]But this is how God demonstrates his own love for us: the Messiah died for us while we were still sinners.

[9]How much more, in that case – since we have been declared to be in the right by his blood – are we going to be saved by him from God's coming anger! [10]When we were enemies, you see, we were reconciled to God through the death of his son; if that's so, how much more, having already been reconciled, shall we be saved by his life. [11]And that's not all. We even celebrate in God, through our Lord Jesus the Messiah, through whom we have now received this reconciliation.

I have heard it said – one hears all sorts of strange things in church – that John's **gospel** is all about the love of God, but Paul's letters are all about **law**, justice and hard, sharp things like that. Well, this passage challenges such a theory head on. In fact, of course, so does John's gospel too: John's vision of God's love is tempered like steel in the furnace of the bitter hostility expressed against Jesus, and the incomprehension of everyone from the **disciples** to the crowds to the chief **priests** to Pilate.

But Paul's vision of God's love, rising here like the sun on a clear summer's morning, shines through all the detail that has gone before. You need to wake up early, to get out of bed, and to throw back the curtains, to see it; that's what the previous four chapters are about. But now that we have done all that, the view is here for us to enjoy.

And to be dazzled by. God's love has done everything we could need, everything we shall need. As Paul continues to explore the meaning of the reconciliation that has taken place between God and human beings, he delves down into the depths of what God had to do to bring it about. But before we can even look at that, there is something strange and powerful in this passage which Paul has not made explicit before, but which creeps up on us almost unawares. It is this: when we look at Jesus, the **Messiah**, we are looking at the one who embodies God's own love, God's love-in-action.

Look at verse 8. What Paul says here makes no sense unless Jesus, in his life and death, was the very incarnation, the 'enfleshment' (that's what 'incarnation' means) of the living, loving God. After all, it doesn't make sense if I say to you, 'I see you're in a real mess! Now, I love you so much that I'm going to . . . to send *someone else* to help you out of it.' If the death of the Messiah demonstrates how much God loves us, that can only be because the Messiah is the fully human being (how much more human can you get than being crucified?) in whom the living God is fully present. Paul has not, in this letter, explained how this comes about. He assumes it. Elsewhere in his letters he says a bit more about it, though still not as much as we might have liked. But it's clear that he believed firmly that Jesus was (as we say) fully divine, and that this wasn't an odd belief, added on to the outside of his thinking, but one of the key elements which tied everything else together.

In particular, it ties together his view of God's love and his view of the Christian hope. Romans 5—8 is, from one point of view, all about hope: the solid, sure hope that all those who belong to God through **faith** in his action in Jesus are assured of final salvation. What this salvation will look like is not Paul's present concern. He will say more about it in chapter 8. At the moment he highlights the point his readers have needed to know ever since 2.1–16: that, when the final judgment comes, they will be rescued.

We should not forget how the picture of **justification** works out in practice. Paul constantly keeps before his mind the past, present and future tenses of God's work. He set out the ultimate future in chapter 2: there will come a day when God will judge all human secrets, and this judgment will be entirely just, fair and impartial. If this sends shivers down our spines – well, it should. But then he has argued in great detail, in 3.21—4.25, that when people believe in God's **good news** about Jesus, they are assured in the present that they already belong to the **covenant** family, the people whose sins are forgiven, who have already received the verdict 'in-the-right' from God's court. We are bound to ask, how does God know? How can it be that people who have the rest of their lives still to lead, lives in which they might do all kinds of wicked things, are nevertheless given this assurance that the future verdict is already known?

A good deal of Romans 5—8 is written in reply to this question (though there are other major themes as well, as we shall see). But the answer begins here: that the Christian hope, for the verdict issued in the present to be reaffirmed in the future, is based securely on what God has already done in the death of Jesus. (Paul returns to this theme, in great exultation, in 8.31–39.) The death of the Messiah on our behalf, when we were weak, helpless sinners (verses 6 and 8), demonstrates how much God loves us; and if he loves us that much, he can be trusted to rescue us from the coming day of judgment (verse 9). After all, God did the unthinkable thing in sending his son to die for us while there was nothing whatever to commend us to him, and indeed everything to make him revolted by us – when, in other words, we were his enemies (verse 10). Now that we are his friends, reconciled to him in the manner described in verses 1 and 2, God is not about to abandon us after all.

The argument thus takes the form, familiar in various systems of logic not least Jewish ones, of a 'how much more'. If God has done the difficult thing, how much more is he likely to complete the job by doing the easy bit. If someone has struggled up a sheer rock face, against all the odds, to get to the top of the mountain, they are not likely to give up when, at the top of the vertical wall, they are faced with an easy stroll on a grassy path to get to the summit itself. If someone has driven to the other end of the country, through rain and snow and freezing fog, to see a friend in need, they are not going to abandon their quest when they arrive at the house, the skies clear, the sun comes out, and all they have to do is walk up the garden path and ring the doorbell. That is the force of Paul's argument in verses 9 and 10.

Verse 11 comes as something of a surprise. The key word, here translated 'celebrate', is the clue. It looks back to what Paul said in 2.17 and 3.27. Those who lived under the law of Moses, as Paul himself had done, 'celebrated' the fact that the creator God was their God. They 'boasted' (the same word can have both a good and a bad sense) that their possession of the law guaranteed them this special status. Paul has shown this celebration to be hollow, this boast to be empty. But in the gospel of Jesus, precisely because it has cut all human pride down to the ground, and because it is embraced in the midst of suffering (5.3), there is reason to say once more, with the Psalmist, 'this God is our God for ever and ever' (Psalm 48.14), and, with Paul himself, 'if God is for us, who can be against us?' (8.31). The fact that this can appear intolerably arrogant, and is indeed bound to appear like that in today's easy-going relativism, should not put us off from embracing it, from the always-surprising celebration of the personal love of God which alone enables us to make those claims.

In fact, the resistance to such claims may well come from

the constant impulse to resist the Lordship of Jesus, the one through whom it is accomplished. Paul lived in a world where other 'lords' reigned supreme, and resented alternative candidates for their position. So do we.

ROMANS 5.12–17
The Big Picture in Shorthand: Adam and the Messiah

[12]Therefore, just as sin came into the world through one human being, and death through sin, and in that way death spread to all humans, in that all sinned . . . [13]Sin was in the world, you see, even in the absence of the law, though sin is not calculated when there is no law. [14]But death reigned from Adam to Moses, even over the people who did not sin by breaking a command, as Adam had done – Adam, who was an advance prototype of the one who would come.

[15]But it isn't 'as the trespass, so also the gift'. For if many died by one person's trespass, how much more has God's grace, and the gift in grace through the one person Jesus the Messiah, abounded to the many. [16]And nor is it 'as through the sin of the one, so also the gift'. For the judgment which followed the one trespass resulted in a negative verdict, but the free gift which followed many trespasses resulted in a positive verdict. [17]For if, by the trespass of the one, death reigned through that one, how much more will those who receive the abundance of grace, and of the gift of covenant membership, of 'being in the right', reign in life through the one man Jesus the Messiah.

The sculptor was pleased with his work. It was a fine statue, and it looked good in the town square. The subject had lived in the little seaport all his life, and had become well known through organizing the coastguard service. This had turned to fame when, at great risk to his own life, he had rescued virtually single-handed a boatload of people caught off the rocks in a winter storm. The town was grateful, and commissioned a statue of him from the sculptor.

But it wasn't long before trouble arrived. The next summer, a gang of noisy youths came to the town for a laugh. They rampaged up the little main street; they broke a couple of windows; they shouted rude words at passers-by. And when they got to the statue, they decided to have some real fun. First they daubed it with red paint. Then they threw stones at it. Then they took it in turns to run, jump and kick it with both feet in the air. After a few minutes of this, the statue, which had not been made to withstand such treatment, snapped off its base and crashed into the road, smashing into pieces. The youths fled, still laughing.

The town council pondered their response, and called in the sculptor. They were determined not to be beaten. They wanted the statue remade exactly as it had been. But the sculptor had a better idea. He would remake it all right – but in a much tougher material. It would look better, too. He wasn't just going to put things back as they had been. This was the opportunity to do something really spectacular.

The story could go on. I like to think of the youths themselves getting into trouble in a boat, being themselves rescued by the coastguard, and coming to their senses. But we have gone far enough for the main point to emerge, which otherwise we might not spot in the middle of Paul's dense and difficult writing. The main point is that what God has done in the one man Jesus the **Messiah** is far, far more than simply putting the human race back where it was before the arrival of sin. The statue has been remade, and it is far more splendid than before. It isn't a case of 'what they knocked down, God will put back up'. Nor is it a case of 'what they did wickedly, God will do graciously'. God has done far, far more. That is the point underlying verses 15, 16 and 17.

The reason Paul gets into this position is that, at last, he is standing back from the argument so far and summing up where he has got to. This means telling the story of Adam and the Messiah. The point of the **covenant** with Abraham, as we have insisted all along, was to undo the primal sin of humankind, the basic idolatry which led to the dissolution and decay of genuine humanness, resulting in death itself. Now Paul has shown that the promises to Abraham are fulfilled in and through Jesus the Messiah, and he has glanced ahead (5.1–11) to see how this works out in terms of the future hope. He is then in a position to sketch the big picture which now emerges, the picture from which he will then develop his account of God's renewed people in chapters 6 and 8.

But 'sketch' is the operative word. More than anywhere else in his writings, Paul allows his mind to go at such a pace that he seems only to write one word for every four or five he really needs if he is to make himself clear. We stumble along behind, trying to make sense of it, and gradually the following picture emerges.

He begins in verse 12 as though he is going to outline a balanced picture: As by one man sin entered the world, so by one man God dealt with sin. But he stops halfway, where you see the three dots at the end of the verse. He has realized that there are two different things that need to be said first, before he can set out this direct balance. The first of these extra things occupies verses 13 and 14; the second is the theme of verses 15, 16 and 17, which we have already glanced at.

Verses 13 and 14 explain a puzzle that might otherwise get in the way. A long time passed between Adam and Moses. Adam was given a direct command, and broke it; God gave Israel a set of direct commands through Moses, and they broke them. But in between the two, in this broad-brush account of early history, human beings went on sinning, and dying, even though there was no law to keep track of what they did. The place and role of the **law** of Moses within the overall rule of sin is very important to Paul, as we shall see in chapter 7 in particular, so it is vital for him that he clear up any potential misunderstandings in this area at the outset.

Verses 15, 16 and 17, as we saw, then insist that putting

humankind to rights is a far, far greater thing than simply a reversal of Adam's sin and its results. The 'trespass' and the 'gift' are not equal and opposite. Death is purely negative. God's gift of **life** cannot simply be compared with it, as though death and new life were simply equal and opposite. The 'negative verdict', the 'condemnation', which followed the original trespass, was the direct result of what had been done; but God took the initiative in a situation where there was nothing but sin to be seen, coming to the place where humankind was in ruins in order to make of his human creatures something far better than they had been in the first place.

Verse 17 takes this contrast in scale to an even greater length. The result of sin was the 'reign of death': death, the ultimate in corruption and dissolution, rules at present over the whole world and everything in it. But, whereas we might have expected the other half of the contrasting pair to be 'the reign of life', Paul goes one further: what we now await is the reign – of those who receive God's gift of covenant membership, of the status of 'being in the right'. Paul does not often speak of the coming 'reign' of those who belong to Jesus (a theme we come across in other early Christian texts such as Revelation 20.4, 6; 22.5). But here, as for instance in 1 Corinthians 6.2, it is quite clear. The 'kingdom of God', that is, God's sovereign and saving rule over the world, is presently exercised through the risen Lord Jesus. But it will be exercised in the future, so it seems, through the fully redeemed human beings, those marked out in the present by God's gift of the status of 'being in the right', of covenant membership.

Paul is now ready to come back to verse 12, where he began, and lay out his straight comparison once more: as through one man, so through one man. But before we move to the next section we should pause and reflect on the astonishing generosity of God's grace. Look back at verses 15, 16 and 17 and see how often the word 'gift' occurs. Have you really grasped the lavish scale of God's generosity?

ROMANS 5.18–21

The Triumphant Reign of Grace

[18]So, then, just as, through the trespass of one person, the result was condemnation for all people, even so, through the upright act of one person, the result is justification and life for all people. [19]For just as through the disobedience of one person many received the status of 'sinner', so through the obedience of one person many will receive the status of 'in the right'.

[20]The law came in alongside, so that the trespass might be filled out to its full extent. But where sin increased, grace also superabounded; [21]so that, just as sin reigned in death, even so, through God's faithful covenant justice, grace might reign to the life of the age to come, through Jesus the Messiah, our Lord.

God has done it; God will do it. That is the message of this dramatic little passage, summing up the whole story of the letter so far.

That might sound strange, since the word 'God' doesn't occur in these verses. But what Paul has done is, if anything, even more effective. In speaking of the result of the act of Jesus in verses 18 and 19, and in speaking of 'grace' in verses 20 and 21, he has pointed towards the God whose saving plan has now been put into effect. Like a good storyteller, he has left us to imagine for ourselves the one who could plan something like this and bring it off, the one whose hidden name is 'grace'.

Instead of a statue being knocked over and replaced, think now of two different statues, facing one another across a town square. The first is a sad, indeed grim figure. It is the death-mask of a once noble character who, through a life of folly and dissipation, bears now on his face the unmistakable signs of decay that result from such a course. The second is all **life** and excitement, looking as if at any moment it might spring from its plinth and do acrobatic tricks out of sheer exuberance. That gives you something of the flavour of the contrast in these verses between the two types of humanity. Paul is going to say

93

much more in the coming chapters about these two types, so it is as well to get to know them as soon as we can.

The first is of course Adamic humanity, the humanity that reflects the 'one man' Adam, whose breaking of God's commandment brought sin and death into the world. (Paul does not discuss, and nor shall we, the question of what actual events lie behind the highly coloured account of Genesis 3. Suffice it to say that the idea of a beautiful and good world, spoiled at one point in time by human rebellion, remains basic to all early Christian, as to all Jewish, thought.) The picture of humankind in a state of sin is indeed a sorry one. Sin brings condemnation (verse 18), the final judgment spoken of in 2.1–16. It means that those who live in the state of sin have the status of 'sinners' (verse 19); they are not, that is, basically good people who sometimes do bad things, but are rather basically flawed people whose flaws reveal themselves repeatedly in specific acts of sin.

By contrast, a new type of humanity has been let loose into the world through the 'upright act' of the one man Jesus the **Messiah**. The word I have translated 'upright' carries all the echoes of 'justice' and '**covenant** faithfulness' which have been such an important part of Paul's argument up to this point. Jesus acted as the embodiment both of God's covenant faithfulness and of the faithful obedience which Israel (3.2) should have offered to God but failed to do. Here Paul is summing up what he said about the Messiah's faithfulness in 3.22. His 'uprightness' (verse 18) and his 'obedience' (verse 19; compare Philippians 2.8) are ways of describing what Jesus did, supremely going to his death, in such a way as to bring out Paul's belief that this was the climax of God's saving plan. When God entered into covenant with Israel, it was so that Israel could be the means of dealing with the evil that had infected God's world. Now, in the Messiah, that purpose has been realized.

The renewed human beings who result from this act are declared to be 'in the right', already in the present, as we have seen; and they are assured of 'life' in the future. This is the meaning of '**justification** and life' in verse 18, and of the status of 'in the right' in verse 19. These verses emphasize, as well, the universality both of Adam's sin and of Jesus' saving act. These things were not done on behalf of one segment of humanity only, but for all, Jew and **Gentile** alike, as Paul has emphasized repeatedly in the previous chapters.

Verse 20, however, introduces a new and different note, in line with a theme we heard frequently in the earlier chapters. Into one segment of the first model of humanity, the Adamic model, there has come a new and disturbing note. 'The **law** came in alongside.' Why has Paul introduced the Jewish law here, and what is he saying about it?

It is a revealing moment. Many Jews at the time, including his own former self, would have seen the law as the beginning of the new model of humanity. Israel was called to be different from the rest of the world; God gave his people the law to make this a reality. As we shall see, there remains a sense in which this is still true. Nothing is straightforward when we are dealing with the law in Paul.

But the point Paul is making is that when the **Torah**, the law, arrived in Israel, so far from marking the start of a new type of humanity, *it merely intensified the problem of the old type.* 'The law came in alongside, so that the trespass might be filled out' (verse 19). It will take Paul half of chapter 7 to explain what he means, but we can sum it up in advance like this, drawing on 5.13–14 as well as the present passage. Sin, in the sense of ordinary human wrongdoing, is by itself like a small colour slide, a photograph or piece of film which by itself you can barely see with the naked eye. What the law does is to put this tiny thing into a projector with a bright light behind it and a big screen in front of it. The law *draws attention to sin, but by itself is powerless to do anything about stopping it.*

Go back to our two statues. The gloomy one, the statue with the death-mask, is carrying a book, in which are written all the

95

faults and failings of which the person was guilty. The face is looking down at the book with a sense of futile horror. But Paul says that 'where sin increased, grace also superabounded'. (Paul here uses a word which, apart from his own other use of it in 2 Corinthians 7.4, is not found elsewhere in ancient Greek; maybe he coined it himself.) The implication is not that God has said that the law does not matter. The implication is that God has found a way of dealing with the law as well, a strange new type of fulfilment. This, too, will be spelled out later, in 8.1–11 and 10.5–9. It is as though the second statue, too, is carrying a book, but its pages are all full of life and colour. How this has happened, Paul will tell us later on.

The final picture, in verse 21, expresses exactly this mood of contrast. 'Sin reigned in death': 'sin', now seen as an abstract power, has taken hold of the world. It has ruled the world the way an evil tyrant rules a country, destroying it bit by bit rather than allow any rebellion, until the whole place is laid waste. But the energy and new life of the alternative model of humanity come bubbling up at us from the second half of the verse. Instead of the reign of sin – a cold, static thing – we have the reign of grace, an energetic rule full of new possibilities. The reign of grace goes forward at speed towards its goal, which is the life of the **age to come**, the time when God will usher in the new creation in which all wrongs will be put to right (see 8.18–25).

(We should note that the normal translation, '**eternal life**', where I have put 'the life of the age to come', gives most modern readers the quite wrong impression that Paul is talking about spending 'eternity' in a world beyond space, time and matter, in '**heaven**'. Paul never mentions such an idea. What he has in mind, here and elsewhere, is the bodily **resurrection** of God's people to share in the new earth and new heavens which will result from God's liberation of the present world from decay and corruption. If there is any doubt about this, chapter 8 will remove it.)

In this final statement of the reign of grace, and hence of the second model of human existence, Paul adds two phrases to indicate how all this surprising new life has been achieved. On the one hand, it is 'through God's faithful covenant justice'. Once again, this word is difficult to translate, but as we look back over the previous chapters it is clear what Paul means. The new world, the new type of human existence, has been brought about because the living God has been faithful to his covenant, the covenant designed to put the world to rights. On the other hand, it has been achieved 'through Jesus the Messiah, our Lord'. The chapter ends, as do almost all the paragraphs in this section (see 5.11; 6.11; 6.23; 7.25; 8.11 and 8.39) by reminding us that what God accomplished in Jesus remains the driving force of the whole thing. In the case of the present chapter, the death of Jesus has been seen as the putting into action of God's love (5.8), and above all as the act of obedience through which, as always envisaged in the covenant, sin and death have been defeated and grace and life unveiled in their place.

The new model of humanity has sprung to life. The question now before us is: at which side of the town square are we living?

ROMANS 6.1–5

Leaving the State of Sin through Baptism

¹What are we to say, then? Shall we continue in the state of sin, so that grace may increase? ²Certainly not! We died to sin; how can we still live in it? ³Don't you know that all of us who were baptized into the Messiah, Jesus, were baptized into his death? ⁴That means that we were buried with him, through baptism, into death, so that, just as the Messiah was raised from the dead through the father's glory, we too might behave with a new quality of life. ⁵For if we have been planted together in the likeness of his death, we shall also be in the likeness of his resurrection.

Everybody knows Jesus' spectacular story of the Prodigal Son (Luke 15.11–32). The younger son twists his father's arm for his share of the property, goes off and spends it all, and comes home, he thinks, in utter disgrace. Then, to his astonishment, he finds his father running down the road to meet him, and throwing a huge party in his honour. He is welcomed back as a son, even though he doesn't deserve it (and even though his older brother grumbles).

Now come forward a year or two, and imagine a thought stealing unbidden into the young man's mind. Life has settled down to a reasonably humdrum existence again. His older brother tolerates having him around, more or less; his father is getting older. He remembers with a happy sigh the day he came up the road and his father came running to greet him ... And he thinks, supposing I did it again? Why not help myself to enough things to survive, run away for a few weeks, and then play the penitent and come back again? Maybe I'll get another party!

Absurd? Unthinkable? Don't you believe it. It's exactly what a great many people think. 'God will forgive me; that's his job!' declared a famous philosopher two centuries ago. And a great many people today seem to believe that the *only* **word** the church should say to anyone is the **message** of forgiveness. I was asked on a radio programme only the other day, 'Surely for a church that believes in tolerance it's going to be difficult to lay down a moral law?' We must, as the phrase goes, be 'inclusive'; we must tell people that God accepts them exactly as they are. Sometimes this is backed up with a version of what Paul has just been saying: where sin abounded, grace abounded even more. So – the only thing to say to someone who sins is, 'That's fine, God loves you!'

I suspect that Paul had met exactly this line of argument – probably again and again. With one difference: I doubt if anyone had seriously been proposing to him that, since God's love reaches us while we are still sinners, we should stay as 'sinners' in order that God's love may go on reaching us. I suspect he had met the line of thought in the form of people objecting to his doctrine of God's free grace: 'You can't go around saying that! People will think they can do what they like!' In fact, as we saw in 3.8, some people do seem to have accused him in more or less that way.

Chapter 6 is written, at one level at least, to answer this point. But it isn't only an aside, as though Paul were simply taking time out of the main flow of thought to deal with a particular problem. He uses the question, as a wrestler uses the force of his opponent's attack, to advance the main thing he wants to say. At this point we go back, not to one of Jesus' stories, but to a much larger and older one. Think of the second book in the Bible, the book Exodus.

Exodus tells the story of how the children of Israel were enslaved in Egypt. God heard them crying in the misery of slavery and oppression, and God sent Moses to bring them out and away to freedom in the promised land. They came through the Red Sea, leaving behind the land of slavery and discovering a new freedom. God led them to Mount Sinai, where they were given the **law**. They then spent . . . well, somewhat longer than they had imagined, wandering round the wilderness and grumbling against God. But he continued to lead them by his own presence, in the pillar of cloud and fire, until eventually they entered the land they had been given as an inheritance.

This story is well enough known. What is not normally recognized is that, here in Romans, Paul tells a version of the very same story, starting with this present passage. Romans 6 describes how Christians come through the water of **baptism** (like the Red Sea) and thus leave behind the land of slavery and enter upon a new freedom (like leaving Egypt and setting off for the promised land). Romans 7 wrestles with the question of what happened at Mount Sinai and the problems that resulted, leading to a strange new fulfilment of the law. Romans 8 describes the Christian life in terms of God leading his people home to their inheritance, which turns out to be the whole redeemed creation – and Paul warns against precisely the kind of grumbling of which the Israelites had been guilty ('You don't want to go back to slavery, do you?' he asks in 8.15).

Why has Paul done it like this? I think there are three reasons, which work together.

First, he has not forgotten (even if we may have done!) that what God has accomplished in Jesus is the fulfilment of the promises made to Abraham. But in Genesis 15, the chapter Paul expounded in Romans 4, God promised Abraham that, after a period of slavery, he would lead Israel out and home to their own land. Romans 6, 7 and 8 are a way of saying: this is what God was really promising to Abraham. This is the ultimate fulfilment of the **covenant**. This is how the world is to be put to rights, as God always intended.

Second, many Jews of Paul's day were in fact thinking in terms of a 'new **Exodus**', a great new act of God through which Israel would be freed from oppression. Paul agrees with this expectation, but instead of seeing it in terms simply of political freedom from Rome, he translates it into the ultimate freedom: the liberation of the whole cosmos from sin, corruption and death.

Third, he is thereby deliberately highlighting the fact that what God has done in and through Jesus the **Messiah** is the true fulfilment of the hope of Israel. It is not that Israel and its hope have been left behind as an earlier stage of the plan. On the contrary: the salvation which God has accomplished in the Messiah, the salvation which he will complete by the **spirit**, is the goal of all that had gone before. And this, as we shall see at the beginning of chapter 9, raises in the most acute form possible the further question, which has been in Paul's mind since at least the start of chapter 3: what then are we to say about continuing ethnic Israel? Chapters 6, 7 and 8 are thus designed *both* as a spectacular exposition of the Christian life in their own terms, *and* as a way of taking forward the thrust of the whole book of which they form a central part.

So what is Paul's answer to the extraordinary suggestion in the first verse? What would he say to someone who declared that since God accepts us as we are, it is better not to change the way we are, since God has affirmed it as good?

His answer is that in becoming a Christian you move from one type of humanity to the other, and you should never think of yourself in the original mode again. More particularly, in becoming a Christian you *die and rise again with the Messiah*. Here we meet, for the first time in Romans, one of Paul's central beliefs: that since the Messiah represents his people, what is true of him is true of them. That is why he speaks of people coming 'into the Messiah', or being 'in the Messiah', or of things happening to them 'with the Messiah'. These are not accidental verbal tricks. You cannot substitute the name 'Jesus' for 'Messiah' in sentences like that. (Of course, Paul believes that Jesus was and is the Messiah; but my point is that the logic of what he is saying works on the assumption that, as Messiah, he is not just a private individual, Jesus of Nazareth; he is the 'anointed one', who sums up his people in himself.)

More particularly, the act of baptism, which as far as Paul was concerned was the practical and physical beginning of the Christian life, involves the Christian in *dying and rising with the Messiah*. Here and elsewhere, Paul understands baptism partly in terms of the Exodus to which John's baptism looked back, partly in terms of Jesus' own baptism by John, but more particularly in terms of the 'baptism' of which Jesus himself spoke (Mark 10.38), that is, his death. When people submit to Christian baptism, they die with the Messiah and are raised with him into a new **life**.

This means, first and foremost, a change of status. We are no longer located 'in sin'; grace has met us there (5.8; 5.20), not in order to tell us that we were all right as we were, but in order to rescue us and take us somewhere else. Paul uses the image of planting, as with a tree or a shrub. Once you've been planted in a particular soil, that is where you must grow. In baptism, you are planted into the death of Jesus, in order that you may now live as a renewed human being, planted also in his **resurrection** life.

Living in accordance with a change of status requires that you recognize it and take steps to bring your actual life into line with the person you have become. When someone gets married, they may well not feel very different, but a change has occurred to which they must now conform. Promises have been made; those promises can be broken, but they can't be unmade. In many cultures, when the father of a family dies, the oldest son must assume responsibility as the head of the family, whether or not he wants to do it or feels up to the task. That is his new status, and he must live up to it as best he can.

Once you are baptized, of course, you can try to shirk or shrug off your new responsibilities. You can pretend you don't after all have a new status. Paul addresses that kind of problem in 1 Corinthians 10. But what you can't do is get unbaptized again. Don't even think of trying to go back to Egypt. Better think carefully about who you now are, and set off for the promised land.

That is, more or less, what Paul will now go on to say. But pause first, and reflect. If you have been baptized, what does it mean to you? Should you be exploring its significance a bit more? If you haven't been baptized, is it time to think about it?

ROMANS 6.6–11

Dead to Sin, Alive to God

[6]This is what we know: our old humanity was crucified with the Messiah, so that the solidarity of sin might be abolished, and that we should no longer be enslaved to sin. [7]A person who has died, you see, has been declared free from all charges of sin.

⁸But if we died with the Messiah, we believe that we shall live with him. ⁹We know that the Messiah, having been raised from the dead, will never die again. Death no longer has any authority over him. ¹⁰The death he died, you see, he died to sin, once and only once. But the life he lives, he lives to God. ¹¹In the same way you, too, must calculate yourselves as being dead to sin, and alive to God in the Messiah, Jesus.

From time to time I hear of someone who has suffered a bad accident, or a particular kind of illness, and can no longer remember who they are.

It must be deeply disturbing – both for the person concerned and for those trying to help. We are so used to people knowing their own name, where they live, what job they do, who their family are, and so on, that the thought of talking to someone who genuinely can't remember any of these things is alarming. Taking it back a stage further, there are those even more rare occasions, verging off into legend, when a child who has been lost as a baby is found some years later, having been brought up by animals, without any idea even of what a human is, let alone that they themselves are human.

Faced with one of these situations, what we long to be able to do is to help the person concerned to discover who they are so that they can bring their lives back into line with their actual identity. People who suffer memory loss can often be eased back, bit by bit, into normal life, into finding their way around once more. The child brought up in the jungle can discover overnight all kinds of undreamed-of human possibilities, such as articulate speech. Paul's aim in this passage is to do something of the same sort with people who need to learn, or at least to be reminded, of the new identity they have as baptized Christians.

The basic move he makes is to place them on the map he drew towards the end of chapter 5, and to insist that they belong on one side of it rather than on the other. You remember the map: there are two types of humanity, those in Adam and those in the **Messiah**. We all began life 'in Adam', and, if we're honest, it often feels as though we are still there (particularly, I think, if you have been a Christian for some time, and have forgotten what it actually felt like to be ignorant of God's love and forgiveness). But Paul insists that we are not. When Christians say, as they sometimes do, that they did something wrong because of the 'old Adam' or the 'old man' still at work in them, they are going against what Paul states explicitly in this passage: that the 'old humanity' was crucified with Jesus. The Adamic life had its own solidarity, bound fast in a network of sin, enslaving all its occupants as surely as Pharaoh enslaved the Israelites. And the point of being crucified is that once you're dead you can no longer be enslaved in that way. As Paul explains in verse 7, once you're dead, sin has no more claim on you. You are free from all charges.

So where does that leave us? In a kind of no man's land, half way between Adam and the Messiah, neither dead nor alive? No. Paul insists that we are now 'in the Messiah', so that what is true of him is true of us, however unlikely it sounds and however much it doesn't yet feel true. And what is true of the Messiah, ever since the glory of Easter day, is that he is alive again with a **life** death cannot touch. He hasn't come back into the same life, as did Jairus' daughter, Lazarus and those others raised by Jesus (and for that matter by Elijah and Elisha). He has gone on, through death and out the other side into a new bodily life beyond the reach of death – a concept we find difficult to grasp but about which the early Christians are very clear. Paul's point is that, if we are 'in the Messiah', then that is where we are, too.

Of course, we are not yet bodily raised as one day we shall be. That remains in the future. That future is secure and certain, as Paul says in 8.11 and in the entire argument of 1 Corinthians 15, but it remains in the future none the less. But part of the point of being a Christian is that the future has come forward into the present in the person and achievement of Jesus, so that his followers already taste the reality of that future while living in the present. The Christian stands on **resurrection** ground. We are not 'in Adam', we are 'in the Messiah', the one who died and is now alive for evermore.

Paul declares that we must 'calculate' this (verse 11), or, in the more familiar translation, that we must 'reckon' it. This has often been seriously misunderstood. People have sometimes supposed that Paul was referring to a fresh leap of **faith**, a leap by which we might attain a new kind of holiness, beyond the reach of temptation and sin. That might be very desirable for anyone – one hopes, most Christians – who, still troubled by sin, is eager to leave it behind. But this is not what Paul is talking about.

The word he uses is a word used in bookkeeping, in calculating accounts, in working out profit and loss figures. Now of course when you do a calculation you get an answer which, in a sense, didn't exist before. But in another sense all that the calculation does is to make *you* aware of what *in fact* was true all along. It doesn't create a new reality. Until you add up the money in the till, you don't know how much your day's takings were worth. But adding it up doesn't make the day's takings a penny larger or smaller than they already are.

Paul is telling us to do the sums, to add up, to work out the calculation – not to screw up our spiritual courage for a fresh leap of faith in which we imagine ourselves to be actually sinless. And here is the point. It is often hard to believe the result of the calculation. But faith at this point consists, not of shutting one's eyes and trying to believe the impossible, but opening one's eyes to the reality of Jesus and his representative death and resurrection – and to the reality of one's own standing as a baptized and believing member of Jesus' people, those who are 'in the Messiah'. That is the challenge of verse 11. We need to remember who we really are, so that we can act accordingly.

A well-known illustration makes this point exactly – one

which, though I have known it for a long time, has just recently been echoed in real life for someone I know. Imagine renting a house from a landlord who turns out to be a bully, always demanding extra payments, coming into the house without asking, threatening you with legal action or violence if you don't give in to his demands. You get used to doing what he says out of fear. There doesn't seem to be any way out.

But then, to your relief, you find somewhere else to live. Someone else pays off your remaining rent and you can leave. You move out and settle in the new place. But, to your horror, a few days later the old landlord shows up at the door and barges into the house. He is angry and demands more money. He threatens to take you to court. The old habit returns: you are strongly tempted to pay him what he demands, just to get him to leave. But you know you are not his tenant any more. You have seen the paperwork; his final bill was paid; nothing more is owing. Trembling, you get up and tell him to leave. He has no claim over you.

Depending on how unpleasant a character the landlord is, you may or may not have to call the police. But Paul's appeal in verse 11 is exactly like that. Remind yourself of the paperwork, he says. Remember who you really are. Don't give in to the voices that tell you you are still in Adam after all, and should be behaving just like you used to. Resisting temptation isn't a matter of pretending you wouldn't find it easier to give in. It's a matter of learning to think straight, and to act on what you know to be true.

ROMANS 6.12–14

The Call to Holy Living

[12]So don't allow sin to rule in your mortal body, to make you obey its desires. [13]Nor should you present your limbs and organs to sin to be used for its wicked purposes. Rather, present yourselves to God, as people alive from the dead, and your limbs

and organs to God, to be used for the righteous purposes of his covenant. [14]Sin won't actually rule over you, you see, since you are not under law but under grace.

We ended the last section with a picture of someone moving house, changing from one landlord to another. Let's extend that a bit, and imagine that I am a smallholder living out in the countryside, about a thousand years ago. My little farm sits on the border between two great estates, and for years the lord of the manor in whose land I actually live has had me completely under his thumb. In particular, whenever he has wanted to fight a war or even a local skirmish he has called on me to join up and fight on his side, and has threatened me with all sorts of unpleasant things (like burning my house down, for instance) if I don't come along. What's more, he has more than once made me get all my farm implements, nice peaceful things like hoes and spades, and take them down to the blacksmith to make them into swords and shields. So off we go to fight his wars, when really I ought to be looking after the farm.

Well, eventually I saw the light and moved just across the river into the other great estate. We built a new house, brought all our stuff across, and settled down (fortunately my old landlord was away at the time or he'd have tried to stop me). The noble lord who owns the land where I now live gave us a wonderful welcome, and charges us a lot less rent than the other one. From time to time my old boss has come down and threatened to send his henchmen across and do, yes, all sorts of unpleasant things to me once more, but I think he's secretly afraid of my new landlord. I get on with my work and look after my farm. And my new master gets me to help with his work, which is quite different from the battles my old boss used to drag me into. My new master is building schools and hospitals, especially for the really poor people, and sometimes he asks me to bring my tools and help in the work. And if someone's in special need – a death in the family, a fire, animals sick, whatever – he asks me to help out in this way or that. Sometimes of course it's an effort, but I'm glad to do it, especially for him.

A harmless fiction (I quite like living in the Middle Ages on paper, but I'm sure I wouldn't have liked it in reality), but it makes the point at which these verses are driving. What is involved in becoming a Christian, and then living the life of God's renewed humanity, is a change of master.

This all seems very odd to some people. There are many today – as there were probably many in Paul's day, since he finds it necessary to stress this point – who simply don't think in these terms. There are many who treat the Christian **gospel** as just a new way of being religious, without seeing the radical demands it makes on every aspect of life. But there is no neutral ground. Bob Dylan declared (in his Christian phase, I take it) 'You've gotta serve somebody'. 'It may be the devil,' the song went on, 'or it may be the Lord, but you've gotta serve somebody.' Well, Paul doesn't mention the devil at this point, but when he talks about 'sin' there is a sense of a a suprahuman power, a force or energy which is more than the sum total of unhelpful instincts and wrong actions.

This force can and does act like a tyrannical landlord, making demands and backing them up with threats. You *must* live like this: you *must* go out and get drunk; you *must* indulge your sexual appetites as fully as you can; you *must* help yourself to other people's property; you *must* develop new types of weapons to kill more and more people; you *must* extend your business empire as far as you possibly can . . . the list is endless, as it was in Paul's day. And here come the threats: if you don't live like this, you're missing out on real life; you'll never be satisfied until you give in; you'll get sick or stale; people will laugh at you; your economy will crumble; your enemies will take advantage of you. Whenever someone says, 'Oh, but I couldn't possibly give *that* up,' it may be that they have a sober and realistic view of the necessities of life, but it is quite likely that they are simply afraid of the threats of the old landlord.

Perhaps the most important word in this little section is the first one: 'So'. Or you could translate it 'Therefore'. This passage joins on to the previous one, where Paul urged his readers to remind themselves, to calculate and work out, where they now lived. They have crossed the river. They don't belong in the old territory any more. They are not only under no obligation to obey the old landlord; they are under a new obligation *not* to obey him, but to obey the new one instead. And the main weapon they have in that particular battle is to remind themselves of who they are through **baptism** and **faith**. Martin Luther, when tempted and tested inside and out, used to shout *Baptizatus sum!* 'I have been baptized!' That (rather to the surprise of many Christians who suppose Paul, and indeed Luther, would have been wary of such a claim) is the ultimate basis for the new stand.

In particular, Paul envisages the various parts of the human body as implements to be used in the service of this master or that. Our limbs and organs, and for that matter our mind, memory, imagination, emotions and will, are to be put at the disposal not of sin, but of God. We are to think and act as people who have come through the river and out the other side; that is, who have died and been raised to new **life**. We should not miss the powerful implication of this, backed up in more detail at several points in the first letter to the Corinthians. What we do in the present time, when we offer our whole selves to God's service, is the beginning of **resurrection** life. Of course, there will be an enormous change when the resurrection itself occurs (as Paul assures us it will, in 8.11 and elsewhere). Our present bodies will decay and die. But when we are raised, then, no doubt to our great surprise, the work we have done in the present, in the service of the new master, will turn out to be part not only of who we are, but of the new world he will have brought into being. Present yourselves to God, says Paul, as people who are alive from the dead.

Verse 14 adds a different note, reminding us of a theme which, as so often, *we* might have forgotten but Paul has not. One of the reasons sin will not rule over you – one of the reasons the old landlord has no authority over you – is that when you left his territory you also left behind the place where the **law** rules. Think back to 5.20–21. There are two spheres, two places to live, the Adam-humanity and the **Messiah**-humanity. Shockingly, God's law appears to be part of the Adam-world rather than the Messiah-world. How this can be Paul will take the whole of chapter 7 to explain. But for the moment, just in case anyone might think that embracing the Jewish law would help them in serving the new master, Paul rules it out. You are under the rule of grace, not of the law; that is, under the direct and generous rule of God, through the death and resurrection of his son.

One of the lies of the old master, of course, is that the new master is himself really a tyrant, is really out to cramp your style and make you live a shrunken, futile kind of existence. All those 'don't do this, don't do that' rules! One of the most important reminders of who we are and where we live as Christians is that the God we now serve is the God whose middle name is Jesus; the God, in other words, whose very character is grace, generous love.

ROMANS 6.15–19

The Two Types of Slavery

[15]What then? Shall we sin, because we are not under law but under grace? Certainly not! [16]Don't you know that if you present yourselves to someone as obedient slaves, you really are slaves of the one you obey, whether that happens to be sin, which leads to death, or obedience, which leads to final vindi-cation? [17]Thank God that, though you once were slaves to sin,

you have become obedient from the heart to the pattern of teaching to which you were committed. [18]You were freed from sin, and now you have been enslaved to God's covenant purposes ([19]I'm using a human picture because of your natural human weakness!). For just as you presented your limbs and organs as slaves to uncleanness, and to one degree of lawlessness after another, so now present your limbs and organs as slaves to covenant justice, which leads to holiness.

One of our newspaper columnists came up with a bright idea for achieving two purposes at once.

British society (in common with many others in the Western world) is facing a worrying rise in youth crime. Many young people have no jobs, no purpose in life. They have plenty of energy, but not much money and no chance to do and enjoy the kind of things they see on the television. So they turn to crime – and become hard-working experts at all kinds of skills, both physical and mental. We do not, it seems, have very much idea as a society how to cope with this problem. Labelling such people as criminals, and locking them up, doesn't seem to be doing much good.

At the same time, many people in England lament the fact that our cricket team never quite manages to perform up to expectations. We have succeeded in other sports from time to time, but (at the time of writing) it is a long time since English cricket, once the pride and joy of the country, did as well as it should.

Very well, suggested the columnist. Here is the answer. Take those energetic but dangerous young men off the streets. Put them, by all means, in some kind of detention centre. But let their regime be, quite simply, that they are trained to perform on the sports field. Compulsory physical training, learning all the skills of the sport, endless time to practise; before too long we should have a new generation of cricketers ready to take on the world. He didn't add, though he might have done, that since Australia is England's greatest enemy in cricketing terms, there is a certain appropriateness in this method of selection. After all, as Australians themselves frequently remark, their ancestors – deported criminals – were selected by the finest magistrates in London.

Joking apart, the point of the illustration is that all the energy and initiative which at present is going into crime needs not to be squashed but to be channelled in a good direction. 'Just as you presented your limbs and organs as slaves to uncleanness, so now present them to God as slaves to his covenant purposes' (verse 19). There is a sharp challenge there for Christians in every age and generation, not least those who have come to **faith** as adults. Think of the ways in which, in your former life, you employed a lot of energy in going after things which you now regard as wrong. Are you using that same energy, imagination and initiative in working for God's **kingdom**, in extending his **covenant** purposes in the world?

This challenge is the sharp edge of the contrast, in this passage, between the two types of 'slavery'. Paul is eager to ward off any suggestion that, because as Christians we are free from the slavery of sin, this gives us the 'freedom' to do anything that comes into our heads. This is, once more, a charge he must have met quite often, not least from Jews and Jewish Christians who, on hearing that he regarded Christians as free from the **law**, worried quite naturally that they would cast off all moral restraint. (It is amusing to think of Paul facing this charge when in our own day he is often seen as a stern moralist.) Paul knows that the freedom which the Christian enjoys is not that kind of thing – just as the freedom you enjoy when you pass your driving test and have 'the freedom of the road' does not mean that you are free to drive as fast as you like through towns and villages, or to drive on the wrong side of the road, or to drive on railway tracks or across ploughed fields. With new freedoms, you always get new frameworks; the frameworks constrict one kind of freedom (the freedom to do anything at all) in order to enhance another kind (if everybody drove wherever they pleased nobody would be free to drive anywhere very much).

Paul expresses this sense of a new framework by speaking, in quite a dramatic fashion, of a new 'slavery'. Freedom is not a moral vacuum; it has been purchased for us by the death of our sovereign one, Jesus himself. Precisely as free people, and in order to maintain this freedom, we owe him our allegiance. We should not imagine that both kinds of 'slavery' are the same sort of thing, but it is as well to begin by seeing both worlds in terms of obedience to a master. (The sentence in brackets at the start of verse 19 is probably Paul's way of admitting that calling the new life a form of 'slavery' does sound a bit confusing, but that he needs to do it to make the point.)

So Paul lines up the two types of 'slavery'. As he does so, he is constantly using slightly different terms, so if we're not careful the passage can seem a bit bewildering. In verse 16 he speaks of being obedient either to sin or to 'obedience' itself – strange to think of being obedient to obedience, but he needs something to contrast with 'sin' and this will do for the moment. Obedience to sin leads to death, as he has said many times; obedience to 'obedience' leads to 'vindication', the verdict 'in the right' at the final judgment, as in 2.1–16.

The word for 'the verdict, "in the right"' is our old friend 'righteousness', though that is such a difficult word, in contemporary English and in theological debate, that I have done my best to avoid it in this book. It comes back again in verses 18 and 19, where I have translated it 'covenant purposes' and 'covenant justice'. It's a term which can, as you see, cover several different shades of English meaning. Its underlying stress is on the good purposes of the creator to bring the world back from chaos into proper order, and to bring human beings into the right shape and the right relation to himself. Here Paul uses it to indicate that the purpose of the new life, the reason why new standards of behaviour are required, is because God is putting the world to rights, and wants and needs his newborn children to be part of that work, both in their own lives and in their service for his kingdom.

At the centre of the picture we get a glimpse of how the new slavery works in practice. It isn't a matter of new commandments being hurled at us and of our somehow having to try to obey them. A change of heart has occurred (verse 17). Paul spoke much earlier of the problem with Adamic humanity being located not least in the human heart (1.21, 24). Now, though he has not yet explained this in the present letter, he envisages Christians as people who have been transformed from within. There is a fundamental willingness to conform to 'the pattern of teaching to which you were committed'. The early Christians developed certain basic traditions, about the **gospel** itself (1 Corinthians 15.3–8), about the **eucharist** (1 Corinthians 11.23–26), about behaviour (1 Thessalonians 4.1, and our present passage), and probably about several other things as well. These rules of thumb set out a framework for belief and behaviour, a family code of practice. As a pastor, Paul had no doubt often observed that when people became members of the family something happened to them, deep down inside, which made them want to live in line with this community to which they now belonged. Of course it would take teaching and moral effort. But the will was there, and Paul thanks God for it.

It is sobering to imagine what Paul might say if he were to look up for a moment from writing this letter and glance round the church at the start of the twenty-first century.

ROMANS 6.20–23

Where the Two Roads Lead

²⁰When you were slaves of sin, you see, you were free in respect of covenant justice. ²¹What fruit did you ever have from the things of which you are now ashamed? Their destination is death. ²²But now that you have been set free from sin and enslaved to God, you have fruit for holiness. Its destination is the life of the age to come. ²³The wages paid by sin, you see, are

death; but God's free gift is the life of the age to come, in the
Messiah, Jesus our Lord.

One of the things you have to learn when you move house is
which roads lead where. I was Christmas shopping the other
day in the new town where we have just settled, and as I drove
out of a car park I saw a long queue of cars backed up down the
main road. Eager to get home, I saw a side street which led, so
it seemed, across town in the direction I wanted to go. I took it,
only to discover it led into a cul-de-sac. Ah, but there was a
small street leading off at the very bottom. I took that. It turned
out to be a loop, bringing me back where I'd started.

It could have been worse. I once took what looked like a
promising country lane, only to find myself getting stuck, miles
out in the country, in a stream that had burst its banks and
washed away part of the road surface. I have sometimes been
tempted to ignore 'Danger' signs when driving near military
ranges, and to take what would otherwise be the obvious route
across the moors. And of course one can imagine situations
worse again, such as trying to beat the traffic by driving through
a line of road cones, only to discover that the bridge you find
yourself on hasn't been finished yet and you are about to drive
off the end and fall into the river.

The point is obvious, but when it comes to Christian ethics
it is often missed. The rules and guidelines for Christian living
are not there because God happens to like squashing people
into a particular shape whether or not it's good for them,
whether or not it will make them happy. The rules are there
because they are the rules of the road, and it matters which road
you take. One road will ultimately lead you not just into a
cul-de-sac but into disaster. The other road leads you to **life**, life
in a new dimension, life in all its fullness.

This, too, is easy to misunderstand. People have often
supposed that the threat of ultimate death, and the promise of
ultimate life, work simply on the principle of the carrot and the

stick. God, on this model, treats us like ignorant donkeys, waving carrots over our noses ('**Eternal life**! How about that! Now then, get a move on!'), or, if we seem reluctant, giving us a swish with his stick ('You'll feel ashamed! You'll die! Don't do it!'). Maybe it does feel like that sometimes, but, if so, it's probably because we are looking at it wrongly. The point is quite different. As we saw in chapter 1, if you choose to live in certain ways you are choosing behaviour which is, in its own character, destructive both to those who practise it and to those whose lives are affected all around. If (to take an obvious example) people regularly get drunk and go around smashing things up, they are damaging themselves and the world around. It isn't so much that some arbitrary standard declares that such behaviour is wrong and deserves punishment. Such behaviour already shows the signs of its destination. It has the smell of death already upon it. The ultimate punishment is not arbitrary, like putting someone into prison for failing to pay a tax bill. It is much more like what happens when someone drives recklessly over a cliff and falls to their death.

Conversely, when people behave in the patterns set out in the **gospel** and the early Christian teaching, there are signs of life already at work. The life of the **age to come** is not an arbitrary reward, like someone being given a medal for rescuing a child from drowning. It is much more like the reward that a father receives when the child he has rescued is his own beloved daughter.

Pause for a moment and examine that phrase, 'the life of the age to come'. We met it before, at the end of chapter 5. It is often translated 'eternal life', and it clearly sums up Paul's view of the ultimate destination of God's people. But it is often misunderstood. Many people bring to the New Testament an assumed view of the final destination, '**heaven**'. They think of sitting on clouds playing harps, perhaps; and though they perhaps know that's only a picture they still think of the reality in terms of an existence outside space, time and matter. But that is certainly not the New Testament picture, and it's certainly not Paul's idea of the ultimate destination. As a good first-century Jew – and his Christian theology has not changed this view, only deepened it and filled it out – he believed that there were two 'ages': the **'present age'** and the 'age to come'. The present age (see, for instance, Galatians 1.4) was a time when wickedness continued to rule God's world. In the age to come, God's rule would triumph at last. The achievement of Jesus the **Messiah** had brought this 'age to come' forwards into the middle of the present age. Christians were summoned to live in the present in the light of that future, that future which had come to meet them in Jesus. If you want to know what Paul's vision of the ultimate future looked like, peep ahead to Romans 8.18–25. That vision of new creation, not some expectation of a disembodied and timeless 'heaven', is where genuine Christian behaviour will lead.

The future, though, remains God's gift (verse 23). Paul is careful to keep his balance. When you sin, you earn a wage, and the wage is death. But when you live according to God's way of holiness, you do not *earn* the life of the coming age. It remains a free gift, far greater than anything we could have deserved. Final judgment will be in accordance with the life we have led (2.1–16). But it will be 'in accordance with' in the same way that a symphony orchestra playing Beethoven at full blast is 'in accordance with' my feeble attempts to whistle the tune.

Romans 6 is a bracing chapter, one that the church desperately needs to listen to in our own day. It does not give us specific ethical instructions; for those, we must look elsewhere, in this letter and the other early Christian writings. It gives us the framework for thinking about why Christian behaviour matters, and how to put it into practice. People still assume, inside the churches as well as outside, that Christianity is simply a matter of a few strange and restrictive moral rules coupled with a few strange and outdated beliefs and practices. Even a few lines of Paul will put that nonsense to rest, and get us back on track for the serious and necessary business of genuine Christian holiness.

ROMANS 7.1–6

Dying to the Law

[1]Surely you know, my dear family – I am, after all, talking to people who know the law! – that the law rules a person as long as that person is alive? [2]The law binds a married woman to her husband during his lifetime; but if he dies, she is free from the law as regards her husband. [3]So, then, she will be called an adulteress if she goes with another man while her husband is alive; but if the husband dies, she is free from the law, so that she is not an adulteress if she goes with another man.

[4]In the same way, my dear family, you too died to the law through the body of the Messiah, so that you could belong to someone else – to the one who was raised from the dead, in fact – so that we could bear fruit for God. [5]For when we were living a mortal human life, the passions of sins which were through the law were at work in our limbs and organs, causing us to bear fruit for death. [6]But now we have been cut loose from the law; we have died to the thing in which we were held tightly. The aim is that we should now be enslaved in the new life of the spirit, not in the old life of the letter.

I have done my best, in this book and the others like it, to use illustrations which will help my readers get to the heart of the point in each passage. Some reviewers have questioned both the wisdom of this attempt and my skill in achieving it, but I persist. When we come to a passage like this, however, we have a different sort of problem; Paul himself has done what I have been trying to do, and at first sight his illustration (like some of mine, no doubt) doesn't work as well as it should.

The illustration is of a married woman, bound to her husband by the law – or 'the **law**', we could say, because the whole chapter is about the law of Moses, not some other or more

general law. The point Paul seems to be making is that where a
death occurs, it releases people from obligations under the
law, like a married woman who, after her husband's death, is
no longer bound by the law to refuse alternative partners.
But in the second paragraph, verses 4–6, Paul applies this to
Christians, and says on the one hand that *they* died and on the
other that *they* are now free to be married again! What on earth
can he have in mind?

Why is he talking about the law, anyway? You might suppose
that, having written a chapter about Christian behaviour, it
would be quite natural for him to move on to talk about the
law as a source of ethical rules. Many churches, after all, still
have the Ten Commandments written upon the wall; perhaps
(we might think) Paul is moving in that direction. Well, it's true
that he does think the commandments are still important. He
will get to that in 13.8–10, though when he does he will do
more than simply repeat them and insist on obedience. But at
the moment the point is very different. Here the law is part of
the problem, not part of the solution.

You might suppose, if you had been following the argument
of the letter carefully, that he is writing this chapter because
sooner or later he was going to have to tell us what exactly he
meant by all those sidelong references to 'the law' (such as 3.20;
3.27–31; 4.13–15; 5.13–14; 5.20; and 6.14–15). He has hinted
again and again that the law of Moses, though he believes it
was given by God and bore witness to the **gospel** (3.21), nevertheless plays a negative role in God's overall purposes (5.20),
and that the Christian is not 'under the law' (6.14–15). Why
not? According to this view, chapter 7 is written to answer these
residual questions. And it's true that Paul does at last address
them in a fuller way. But that's not the whole story.

Some people simply read Romans 5—8 as a description of
the Christian life. That leads them to suppose that the picture
of moral wrestling in 7.14–25 is a picture of what it's like trying
to lead a Christian life, halfway (as it were) between the bracing

commands of chapter 6 and the final goal as set out in chapter 8. That gives the chapter a role within an overall reading of the section of the letter, but it seems to ignore the fact that the main subject of the chapter is not the Christian life, but the law itself – and that Paul says again and again that the Christian is not 'under the law'.

I think Paul's main reason for writing Romans 7 is that he wants to do two things in particular. He wants to explain what the law was given for, and how in a strange sense it actually did the work God set it up to do, and that it is now, in a new sense, fulfilled through the work of the **Messiah** and the **spirit** (he comes to that in chapter 8) – while at the same time explaining, over against any attempt by Jews or Jewish Christians to suggest otherwise, that the law itself could not give the life it promised, but instead was bound to work on the negative side of the equation. If that sounds complicated, and of course it is, that simply goes to explain why Romans 7, which compresses it all into something like a characteristic Jewish poem of complaint, has proved difficult to understand.

This chapter forms part of Paul's overall strategy, which is to explain to the Roman Christians, many of whom were clearly from a Jewish background (which is why they 'know the law', as in verse 1), the deep-level transition that has been made through the gospel from the **covenant** family defined by the law to the covenant family defined by the Messiah and the spirit. Only if they – and we! – grasp this point will the church be able to understand what God has done and what it now means to share the Christian **faith**, hope and **life**.

The clue to the present passage, which introduces the long discussion of the law, lies in a combination of 5.20 and 6.6. Paul is still thinking in terms of the two types of humanity, Adam and the Messiah; and he understands the Christian as someone whose 'old man' (6.6) has been crucified with the Messiah. Each person is thus to be seen as a composite being, like a woman married to, and hence (in that world at least!) identified with, a husband. And the role of the law is to cement the bond between the person who is 'in Adam' and the 'old man', or 'old Adam', to whom they are 'married'.

This explains verse 4, which is at the heart of this passage. 'You died to the law' refers to the same event as 6.6, where 'the old man' was crucified with the Messiah in order that 'we' might be rescued from the solidarity of sin. Paul is making the striking and controversial claim that the law, when given to Israel, formed a bond between Israel and . . . not God, as one might have supposed, but rather Adam. This explains his otherwise baffling statement in verse 5, and frequently in the rest of the chapter, that the passions of sins were 'through the law' (he means, presumably, 'were aroused through the law', but I have left the translation reflecting his somewhat abbreviated Greek).

The law, then, appears to be part of what is wrong. Given to Israel by God, it reminds Israel constantly that it, too, is 'in Adam'. It does not lift Israel out of the mess. It simply informs Israel that it, too, is in the mess. What that looks like in practice will form the main body of the chapter.

But Paul also gives, in verse 6, an advance sign of the answer. 'We' – that is, of course, those who through **baptism** and faith have been brought into the family defined by the crucified and risen Messiah – we have died to the law (see Galatians 2.19) and so have been cut loose from the ties with which it bound us to the solidarity of the old Adam, forcing us, like a woman bound to a husband, to bear his children, which in this case means death. Instead, we have been bonded to the Messiah in his new, risen life, so that we can bear a different kind of fruit, fruit for God. This is one of the places where Paul draws on the idea of the Messiah as the bridegroom of his people, which emerges again in, for instance, 2 Corinthians 11.2–3 and Ephesians 5.25–27.

He hints, too, at the contrast he mentioned earlier, at the end of chapter 2. Living in the old Adamic solidarity, and within that in Israel under the law, means living the old life under the 'letter' of the law. Living the new life in solidarity with the Messiah means leaving behind every aspect of life in Adam, and being energized in a new way, by God's spirit. Paul has hardly mentioned the spirit up to now (1.4; 2.29; and 5.5 are the only occurrences), but by the end of the present argument he will be ready to write one of the greatest ever accounts of the spirit's work. Perhaps the deepest reason for his writing Romans 7 is that, since God does through the spirit 'what the law could not do' (8.3), it is vital that we see exactly what the law was trying to do and why it was bound to fail. The present chapter, though very difficult, is essential if we are to grasp the depth of the human problem and hence the wonder of God's solution to it.

ROMANS 7.7–12

When the Law Arrived: Sinai Looks Back to the Fall

⁷What then shall we say? That the law is sin? Certainly not. But I would not have known sin except through the law. I would not have known covetousness if the law had not said, 'You shall not covet.' ⁸But sin grabbed its opportunity through the commandment, and produced all kinds of covetousness within me.

Apart from the law, sin is dead. ⁹I was once alive apart from the law; but when the commandment came, sin sprang to life ¹⁰and I died. The commandment which pointed to life turned out, in my case, to bring death. ¹¹For sin grabbed its opportunity through the commandment. It deceived me, and, through it, killed me.

¹²So, then, the law is holy; and the commandment is holy, upright and good.

The house was quiet when the workmen arrived, and when someone came to the door they assumed it was the owner himself. They had come to install a new alarm system on the doors and windows. The owner had been anxious about burglaries, following a spate of break-ins in the neighbourhood, and had called the company to come and set up a better system than his present one.

But the owner was ill on the day the work was to be done, and he had called a neighbour to answer the door while he was out of action. The neighbour went round the house with the workmen, and learned exactly how the alarm system worked. Which gave him an idea . . . and of course put him in an ideal position to burgle the house himself. There was nothing wrong with the alarm system. Indeed, it was excellent. But it put the idea in the neighbour's mind, and enabled him to bring it off.

Another illustration which works up to a point, though not all the way down the line. The picture of the neighbour in this story is actually a composite of 'sin' and 'I' in Romans 7. But it makes the point which is central to Paul's argument throughout: the **law** itself is God's law, and it is holy, just and good. Like the alarm system, it is an excellent thing and in good working order. But if you introduce an error at a different point – if you have an untrustworthy neighbour helping to install it – it will work against you rather than for you.

Before we get to that point, though, we must say a word about this 'I' that figures so large in Romans 7. Many readers have imagined that Paul is simply telling us part of his auto-biography, and the only question then is: Which part? Is he describing the time before he was a Christian? (Some have suggested, for instance, that these verses tell us what it felt like when he reached puberty at the same time as becoming 'a son of the commandment', that is, going through his bar mitzvah, the Jewish ceremony for entering adulthood.) Or is he describing what life is like now that he is a Christian? Or does the chapter move from his pre-Christian life to his Christian life? Or what?

This whole approach is barking up the wrong tree. People in the ancient world often wrote in the first person singular ('I') when they wanted to say something more general. Sometimes English does this with the first person plural ('we'); sometimes, slightly pretentiously, it uses 'one' ('one does sometimes feel . . .'). Paul does it himself in Galatians 2.15–21, with both 'I' and 'we'. There are several good reasons for supposing that this is what he is doing here, rather than transcribing his own struggles with the law. He is not talking about the human race in general. He is talking about Israel in particular – Israel, who received the law as a good gift from God but who found that there was someone lying in wait, like the untrustworthy neighbour in the story, to take advantage of the new gift.

That someone was sin, or perhaps we should say Sin. Israel, too, was 'in Adam'. At the heart of the problem of biblical theology lies the fact that when God chose to redeem the world he called, as his agents, a family which was itself (like everyone else) in need of redemption. We have met this problem in one mode or another several times in the letter. Now we face it head on.

This suggests another reason why Paul might have wanted to say 'I' rather than 'Israel' or 'the Jews'. This was, after all, his story as well. He would certainly not wish to tell it in such a way as to imply that he was not involved in it, was not still grieving over it. There is a direct line, in fact, from the 'I' in this passage, perplexed and distressed over the effects of sin within God's people, and Paul himself in chapters 9–11, in tears over the ongoing effects of sin within the chosen people, his own kinsfolk according to the flesh. The connecting strands between the different sections of the letter are important if we are to understand it as a whole, instead of as a mere collection of short essays. We shall return to this later.

The present passage does two things at the same time. As I look out of my study window, I can see not only what is in the garden outside, but also a reflection of the lamp which sits on the windowsill. If I was to take a photograph of that part of the window, it would record both at the same time, as though they were part of the same view. In the same way, Paul describes the time when the law arrived in Israel in such a way as to reflect, in addition, the time when Adam was given the commandment in the garden (see, again, 5.13–14 and 5.20). His point is that *when God gave Israel the* **Torah**, *Israel copied Adam by breaking it.* Underneath this is the point that 'sin' was latent within Israel all along, so that the effect of the holy and good law was bound to be that Israel broke it. The conclusion Paul draws from this, to our surprise perhaps but fully in line with his own agenda, is that 'the law is holy; and the commandment is holy, upright and good' (verse 12). This chapter is, basically, a way of exonerating the law from blame in the debacle of Israel while simultaneously demonstrating its inability to give what it promised.

What did the law promise? According to verse 10, '**life**'. Again and again, but particularly in passages like Leviticus 18.5 and Deuteronomy 30.15–20, the Torah held out to Israel the promise that those who faithfully observed it would enjoy life, while those who broke it would incur death. Already in the Old Testament a parallel emerges between Israel, given the law and promised the land, and Adam and Eve, placed in the garden and given a commandment with a warning attached: to break this means death. The 'death' in question involved banishment from the garden, just as Israel's punishment ended in **exile**. But this was not the fault of the commandment given in the garden, or of the law given to Israel. It was the result of sin.

Sin, in short, grabbed its opportunity on both occasions. Like the neighbour who might not have thought of burglary had he not witnessed the new alarm system, Israel discovers the power of covetousness by being warned against it (verses 7 and 8). There was a time when the law had not arrived (that strange time between Adam and Moses, of which Paul spoke in 5.13–14). But once the law was given on Mount Sinai, Isael's sinfulness was shown up for what it was. However much the Torah promised life with one hand, the presence and power of sin meant that all it could deliver was death (verses 8–11).

All this raises a question for us which Paul will answer, at least partly, later on. What exactly is this thing called 'sin'? If it is the ultimate problem behind all our other problems, what can be done to defeat it? More especially, what has God done about it? At the moment all we can say is that 'sin' appears to be a force which is essentially opposed to God's creation. It is bent on spoiling the world God made, the humans who reflect his image, and the chosen people called to be the agents of redemption.

Much of this discussion, however fascinating it is in its own terms and within Paul's argument, may seem remote to many modern Christians. Many of us do not often stop to ponder the situation of Israel under the law – though perhaps we should. But the passage has a relevance for us which we should not miss. When we, too, are faced with sin, whether in our own lives or in the wider world, we should not underestimate it. Evil is real and powerful. It is opposed to God, his world, his human creatures, and not least those who are called to follow his son. We dare not trifle with it. It is deceitful. It is deadly.

ROMANS 7.13–20

Looking Back on Life under the Law

¹³Was it that good thing, then, that brought death to me? Certainly not! On the contrary; it was sin, in order that it might appear as sin, working through the good thing and producing death in me. This was in order that sin might become very sinful indeed, through the commandment.

¹⁴We know, you see, that the law is spiritual. I, however, am made of flesh, sold as a slave under sin's authority. ¹⁵I don't understand what I do. I don't do what I want, you see, but I do what I hate. ¹⁶So if I do what I don't want to do, I am agreeing that the law is good.

¹⁷But now it is no longer I that do it; it's sin, living within me. ¹⁸I know, you see, that no good thing lives in me, that is, in my human flesh. For I can will the good, but I can't perform it. ¹⁹For I don't do the good thing I want to do, but I end up doing the

evil thing I don't want to do. [20]So if I do what I don't want to do, it's no longer 'I' doing it; it's sin, living inside me.

Try reading this passage out loud, quickly. Unless you have a very smooth tongue I can guarantee you'll trip up at some point. I remember this being given to a choirboy to read out in church, in an Advent carol service in fact. Poor lad. There ought to be child protection laws against that kind of thing.

There is no denying that the passage is extremely convoluted. It goes to and fro in a manner which, at first glance, seems quite bewildering. Some people have hailed it as a profound insight into the human condition; others have dismissed it as muddled ramblings. My own view is that it is neither of these things. It is not intended as an exact description of Paul's, or anyone else's, actual experience, though it finds echoes in many places both in human life and in literature ancient and modern. That is not the point. Paul is trying, not for the first time, to do at least two things at once.

Having described in the previous passage what happened when the **Torah** arrived in Israel (it meant that Israel copied, and recapitulated, the sin of Adam, showing that Israel was indeed sinful), Paul now moves into the present tense, to describe the actual situation (as opposed to the felt experience) of Israel living under the **law**. What happens when Israel, having been given the law, does its best to live under it?

Some people have seen this as an indictment of Israel, of 'the Jew' trying to earn **justification** or salvation by works-righteousness, to gain favour with God by keeping the law. They have tried to suggest that Paul is showing, in the present passage, what a foolish attempt that was. But that, too, is not the point. Paul exonerates not only the law, but also, interestingly, the 'I': it is no longer 'I' that do it, he says (verses 17, 20), but sin living within me. Not only the law, but Israel itself, appear to be caught up in a larger purpose, a purpose in the service of which they seem for the moment trapped in a negative spiral.

The more Israel does the right thing, which is to embrace God's holy, just and good law (the 'good thing' of verse 13, referring back to verse 12 where the law is described in that way), the more the law itself says: You have broken me.

That is the first thing Paul is doing: to say, in effect, that Israel was right to want to embrace Torah and make it the way of life. But whereas the law was 'spiritual', Israel, the 'I' in the passage, is made of flesh and enslaved to sin (verse 14). Israel belongs, in other words, on the 'Adam' side of the equation. The law does not enable Israel to get out of that problem; it merely intensifies it. So far, so good. We are here on exactly the same ground as in Romans 2.17–24. (In fact, for those with a sharp eye for the symphonic structure of the letter, Romans 7 is a longer version of 2.17–24, while, from one point of view at least, Romans 8 is a greatly expanded version of 2.28–29 – which is why Paul must ask, in Romans 9, the same questions as he asked at the beginning of chapter 3.)

The point of 2.17–24, we recall, was that Israel, though claiming to be better off before God than the rest of the world, not least because of possessing the law, was in fact reduced to the same state as the rest of the world (1.18—2.16), charged before God with sin. Now we begin to see the second point that Paul is making, which is subtle but, to the audience he has in mind, powerful. He has described the problem of Israel under the law so that it looks exactly like the problem which every puzzled pagan moralist from at least Aristotle onwards had observed. There was a long tradition in Greek and Roman philosophy and poetry in which people complained, scratching their heads over it, that they could figure out what was the right thing to do but for some reason or other they couldn't manage to do it. Conversely, they could see with their mind that a certain course of action was wrong, and yet they went ahead and did it anyway. Paul had spent years in the debating halls of the ancient pagan world. He had listened on the street as people quoted snatches of poetry and popular philosophy. Now, as one of his most devastating and clever pieces of writing, so clever that it runs right by a lot of readers to this day, he offers an analysis of Israel's plight under the law which ends up as saying: so this is the height to which God's chosen people attain through their possession of the law – the same height as the puzzled pagan moralist! If anything could demonstrate the problem faced by Israel, this would be it: that however much God's people struggled to obey God's law, they ended up like the rest of the world, in a state of moral incapability.

Paul will himself write a conclusion to this argument in the final section of the chapter. But for the moment we should notice where he has got to. He has exonerated the law from blame in the catastrophe that has overtaken Israel. He has even exonerated the 'I'; there was nothing wrong with being Israel, nothing wrong with wanting to keep God's law (think of Psalms 19 and 119, with their almost mystical longing and love for the law). The real problem was sin.

Paul has already indicated, in a strange little passage in verse 13, what is going to happen to sin. What was responsible for bringing death to 'me', he says, was sin, 'in order that it might appear as sin', and 'in order that sin might become very sinful indeed'. This repeated 'in order that' is itself a bit of a puzzle. Why would God (who is often implicated in Paul's 'in order that' clauses) want sin to grow to full height?

Add to the mix the similar phrase in 5.20: the law came in alongside, *in order that* the trespass might abound. And, for good measure, Galatians 3.22: scripture (i.e. the law) has shut up everything under sin. What was God up to, giving the law not simply *knowing that* it would give sin the chance to grow to its full height, but actually *in order that* it might do so?

We will discover the answer in 8.3, but we must anticipate that moment if we are to see the deepest reason, and one of abiding and indeed shocking relevance for every generation of Christian believers, why Paul has written this chapter the way he has. *God wanted sin to be brought to its full height in order*

129

that he might then deal with it, condemn it, punish it once and for all. But where was sin to grow to full height? Paradoxically, in Israel, the very people God had called to be the light of the world. Why? In order that in the person of Israel's representative, the **Messiah**, sin might be drawn onto one spot and condemned once and for all. What looks at first sight like a tortured and rambling account of personal moral incapacity prepares the way for a statement of the achievement of the cross which is as powerful as anything Paul ever wrote.

ROMANS 7.21–25

The Double 'Law' and the Miserable 'I'

²¹This, then, is what I find about the law: when I want to do what is right, evil lies close at hand! ²²I delight in God's law, you see, according to my inmost self; ²³but I see another 'law' in my limbs and organs, fighting a battle against the law of my mind, and taking me as a prisoner in the law of sin which is in my limbs and organs.

²⁴What a miserable person I am! Who is going to rescue me from the body of this death? ²⁵Thank God – through Jesus our king and Lord! So then, left to my own self I am enslaved to God's law with my mind, but to sin's law with my human flesh.

When you do a complicated mathematical sum, you end up by drawing a line across the page and displaying the result, or, if you like, your 'findings'. The same thing happens after a lengthy judicial review of some complex question. The judge writes a report, ending up with a summary of 'findings'.

That is exactly what Paul does in these closing verses of the chapter. 'This is what I find about the **law**': he uses the language one would use in mathematics or law. That is why, despite a widespread tradition in translations and commentaries, I find it quite impossible to translate 'law' in verse 21 as 'a principle' or 'a law' in the sense of a general truth. The whole argument has been, quite explicitly, about The Law, God's law, the law of Moses; the word 'law' in this verse has the definite article ('the'); only by determining to misunderstand the passage, by deciding that we will force Paul to make a summary statement about something else other than the subject of the rest of the chapter, can we read this passage in any other way.

But what is he 'finding' about the law? He 'finds' that the law has split into two – and that this results in great tension within the 'I' about whom he has been speaking, Israel according to the flesh, Israel living under the law.

He takes the second of these first. I want to do what is right – but there is evil close at hand! Paul here echoes the language used about Cain in Genesis 4.7, and he may be reflecting on the fact that, just as Israel acted out the sin of Adam in 7.7–12, so the moral incapacity revealed in 7.14–20 looks quite like the traditional Jewish picture of Cain. Whether or not that is so, the point here, and in verse 22, is that the 'I' is quite right to delight in God's law. Imagine Paul as a young man praying Psalm 19 or Psalm 119, studying **Torah** prayerfully day and night, longing to wrap it around him like a cloak, to make it his way of life, his every breath. Not only is there nothing wrong with that; it is exactly what Israel was meant to do.

But the closer you hug the law to yourself, if you are still 'in Adam', the more the law is bound to say 'But you're a sinner!' Worse: it will not only accuse, it will tempt, as we saw in verses 8 and 10. It looks as though the law has developed a shadowy copy of itself, a negative identity which seems to be fighting on the side of sin against what the 'I' longs to do. This is an extraordinary thing to say about God's law, but it fits closely with everything Paul has hinted at throughout the letter so far.

How do we hold a paradox like this together? It is never clear – just as many paradoxes are not clear, such as that light can be satisfactorily analysed in terms of waves, or in terms of particles, but that you can't do both at the same time. Maybe things always seem like that when you get close to the heart of mystery. Certainly we should not make life easier for Paul or for ourselves by imagining that 'law' here means something other than God's law, the law given to Israel. If this were not the case, the problem would not be nearly so acute.

The result of the analysis is that the 'I' finds itself a prisoner of war (verse 23). A battle has been going on. The mind of the faithful Israelite (interestingly in view of 1.28) has been engaged on the side of wanting to keep God's law, but sin has been fighting powerfully on the other side, through the Adamic humanity which Israel shares with everyone else. Israel, it seems, has been called to hold on to the enormous tension between being called to be the light of the world and discovering itself to be, like everyone else, soaked in sin. That is the tension in which, at a further stage in the argument, Paul finds himself in Romans 9. And this is why Paul's view of Jesus is so crucial, and why the answer to the question 'Who is going to rescue me?' (verse 24) is that God will, through Jesus the **Messiah**, our Lord. The Messiah sums up in himself *both* Israel according to the flesh *and* the God who comes to the rescue. That will be the point of 8.3–4, and also 9.5.

By this stage someone may be asking, almost angrily: why do we need to know all this? What's the point of Paul writing at such length about the problems of Israel under the law? We live in the twenty-first century, not in the first; most of us in the church were never Jews and have little or no contact with people who are. Surely (they will say) such a central passage as this, in such an important letter, must be about something more relevant?

It's a good question. It is indeed possible to expound passages of scripture in such a way as to make them splendidly irrelevant to Christian readers today, and scholars must always watch out for that danger. But I maintain, on the basis of careful study over a long period, not only that this is the correct way to read this passage, but that exactly in this sense it retains a powerful relevance for Christian readers in any generation and culture. Paul is quite clear that to be a Christian is to be a child of Abraham (Romans 4; Galatians 3). He speaks to ex-pagan Christians about 'our ancestors' when he means the children of Israel who came out of Egypt (1 Corinthians 10.1). If modern Christians forget that they are part of this larger family, stretching back roughly two thousand years behind Jesus, they are cutting themselves off from the root of the tree – the root from which, as new branches, they are claiming to receive **life** (see 11.15–24). It is therefore vital that we know both in what sense there is direct continuity between Israel BC and the Christian church, and in what sense there is clear discontinuity. Many Christians have puzzled over the place of Old Testament law within the life both of the individual Christian and of countries that claim, or try, to be 'officially' Christian. As soon as that sort of question comes up, Romans 7 will be seen to be extremely relevant, even if it is uncomfortable.

In particular, it insists that when God gave the Torah it was not a kind of 'first attempt' at teaching human beings in general the first principles of morality – as though humans needed a few ground rules to get them going, eventually being topped up with the Sermon on the Mount. God's intention was far, far more subtle than that. The problem of evil, the real problem underneath questions both of salvation and of ethics, is far more radical than such an account would imply. When God gave the Torah his intention was to further the purposes for which he called Israel. These purposes were not simply about teaching the world a better standard of morality. They were about rescuing the world from sin and death.

To accomplish this aim, God sent not just his Torah, but also his son and his **spirit**, to do at last what the Torah wanted to do but by itself could not. At which point we turn over the page, ready at last for one of the greatest chapters written by Paul, or any other Christian writer.

ROMANS 8.1–4

God's Action in Messiah and Spirit

[1]So, therefore, there is no condemnation for those in the Messiah, Jesus! [2]Why not? Because the law of the spirit – the one who gives life in the Messiah, Jesus – released you from the law of sin and death.

[3]For God has done what the law (being weak because of human flesh) was incapable of doing. God sent his own son in the likeness of sinful flesh, and as a sin-offering; and, right there in the flesh, he condemned sin. [4]This was in order that the right and proper verdict of the law could be fulfilled in us, as we live not according to the flesh but according to the spirit.

When we lived in the English Midlands, I was once visited by two men researching a potential television programme. There had been a lot of talk about 'Middle England', they said. Since I lived more or less right in the middle of England, what did I think about it?

It was a faintly ridiculous idea, and though we had an interesting chat I never heard what came of it. There is, in fact, a roundabout a few miles south of where we lived, which pretentiously called itself 'Midpoint' or something like that, claiming to be the centre of the country. But of course with a country the odd shape of England there are many different places that could say the same.

When I was teaching undergraduates, I sometimes used to ask them to find a passage which seemed to be right at the centre of Paul's thinking. Like the geographical question, it is impossible to answer, because of the many-sidedness of his writing; but the verses now before us have as strong a claim as any other passage I know. They have a big, thoroughly Pauline picture of God, father, son and **spirit**; they contain one of Paul's clearest ever statements about what was accomplished on the cross; they draw together both his critique of the Jewish **law** and the seeds of his view of how that law is strangely fulfilled in

134

and through the **gospel**; and they hold out the glorious, and typically Pauline, hope that there is indeed 'no condemnation' for those in the **Messiah**. A feast of good Pauline themes, in fact.

Faced with all this richness – not to mention the fact that this passage has been a favourite of many preachers for many years, the source of many prayers and hymns, and was turned into a whole cantata by J. S. Bach – we could be forgiven for being a bit bewildered, and failing to notice the role it plays in the actual argument of the letter, which is of course the primary thing one should always look for before delving into the detail. Though the mood and the tone of voice have changed drastically from the end of chapter 7, the same argument is still in process, as we can see by the continual mention of the law through verses 1–4, and on, in our next passage, to verse 7. The larger argument, in fact, of which chapter 7 forms the first section, continues in chapter 8 as far as verse 11. There we discover how it is that the intention of the law (to give **life**) is finally and gloriously achieved when, by the spirit, God gives **resurrection** life to all those who belong to the Messiah, Jesus. In our present passage the foundation for that conclusion is firmly laid, as Paul unveils (rather as in 3.21) the 'but now' of the gospel, the **good news** which addresses the problems and puzzles that the whole human race, including Israel, would otherwise still face.

This passage, too, opens a whole set of further discussions which take the rest of chapter 8 to address, notably concerned with the work of the spirit. This, in turn, contributes to the great theme of assurance which Paul sums up in the final paragraph (8.31–39), anticipating it in verse 1 with his great shout of triumph which in turn looks back to 5.1–11, and indeed to 5.1–2 in particular. The present passage and the next one (8.1–4 and 8.5–11) stand together as, simultaneously, the conclusion of the argument of Romans 7 and the introduction to the argument of Romans 8. No wonder they are so dense and tight-packed – though not, fortunately, as difficult to unravel as some of Paul's other close writing.

I have often remarked that one of Paul's regular styles of developing an argument is like the opening up of a flower. Out of my window I can see rose bushes. It is winter; they are surrounded by snow; but here and there you can just make out tiny little shoots. At some stage in the late spring they will turn into rosebuds. Then the rosebuds will open and reveal a wonderful flower. And I will think back to the tiny shoots and reflect that the whole rosebud was contained within the shoot, if only I could have seen it.

The present paragraph is an excellent example of this writing style. Verse 1 announces the main point Paul is going to make from now to the end of the chapter: there is no condemnation for those in the Messiah. Verse 2 offers the beginnings of an explanation, but it is so compressed that it will take quite a lot of inspection under a microscope before we can see what exactly it means. No matter; wait for the bud to develop and grow. Verses 3 and 4 open it out so we can see it better. Then verses 5–8 will widen the flower further. Finally, in verses 9–11, the rose will be fully open, releasing its fragrance to all within reach. This should teach us something of how to read Paul: don't stop at a single verse and wonder why it's so dense. See it as part of a larger, growing statement and celebration.

No condemnation! This assurance can of course only carry its full force for someone who has pondered carefully the seriousness of sin and the reality of God's judgment. Anyone who imagined that sin wasn't that serious, or that God wouldn't judge it anyway, would probably shrug their shoulders at Romans 8.1. But then anyone like that probably wouldn't have read this far anyway. The more interesting question about the verse is: why does Paul say 'therefore' at the beginning? Where he left the argument at the end of chapter 7 hardly encourages such a shout of triumph. One might have expected him to say, 'There is therefore a lot of gloom and doom to be faced.'

The answer is not far away, in the string of 'because' sentences that follow in the next verses. Indeed, in the Greek, verses 2, 3, 5 and 6 all contain the little word that means 'because' or 'for', indicating that each step in the argument is *explaining* what has gone before. There is no condemnation, *because* the spirit-law has set you free from the sin-law, *because* God has acted in his son and his spirit to condemn sin and provide life, *because* there are two types of human beings and you are the spirit-type, *because* these two types are heading, respectively, for death and life. There is no condemnation, *because* of all this.

We should not suppose that the word 'law' in these verses means anything other than 'God's law'. Just as in the closing verses of chapter 3 and chapter 7, 'law' is not a 'general principle' or 'system'. Paul revels in the paradox of all this. The spirit has been at work to do what the law wanted to do – to give life, moral life in the present, resurrection life in the future. The law looks on at what God is doing, knowing it hadn't been able to do it itself, but celebrating the fact that God has done it. It is fulfilled (verse 4).

But how can God do this? Will sin, the old enemy, not strike back again? Well, that remains possible, as Paul knew only too well. But sin has received its death-wound. Before the spirit can be unleashed to blow like a spring gale through the dead wood of the world, the power of evil needs to be broken. The way that needs to happen is for sin to be condemned – not just the passing of sentence, but its execution. Paul declares that this is precisely what has happened in the death of God's son, the Messiah. This is one of the points where we hear echoes of almost every chapter in the book, not least of the opening statement of the gospel in 1.3–4.

How does this 'atonement theology' actually work? Paul is writing in great excitement, but also with great precision. First, God sent his own son, which as we saw in 5.8 meant that God has not sent someone else, but has come in person. For the entire passage to make sense, we have to presuppose that by

'God's son' here Paul means, not just Jesus as Messiah (though he means that too; it is vital in his argument) but Jesus as God's own second self. Next, the son came 'in the likeness of sinful flesh'; in other words, to the very point where the problem of chapter 7 had been identified (see particularly 7.14 and 7.25). Sin, as we saw in 5.20 and 7.13, had become 'exceedingly sinful' through the law; God specifically intended that it should. Now Israel, in whom that increase of sinfulness had occurred, was summed up in one man, the representative king, the Messiah. The weight of the world's sin was focused on Israel; the weight of Israel's sin was focused on the Messiah. And the Messiah died a criminal's death, with 'King of the Jews' written above his head. At that moment, God condemned sin. He condemned sin 'in his flesh'. He had cornered it and condemned it. As the prophet had said, 'the punishment that brought us peace fell upon him; and with his stripes we are healed' (Isaiah 53.5).

Notice two things about the way Paul says this. He does not say that God condemned Jesus, but that he condemned *sin* in the flesh of Jesus. He can say other similar things, too (e.g. 2 Corinthians 5.21; Galatians 3.13) but this is his clearest statement. And he also draws in a different image, that of the **sacrifice** for sins in the Old Testament, the specific sacrifice known as the sin-offering. Why?

In the Old Testament, the sin-offering is the sacrifice used when someone has committed sin unwittingly (not knowing it was wrong) or unwillingly (knowing it was wrong but not intending to do it). Paul has analysed the plight of Israel under the law in such a way that it falls exactly into these categories. 'The good I want to do, I don't do; the evil I don't want is what I do.' The 'miserable person' of 7.24 is answered by God's provision of the sin-offering in 8.3, just as, at a more general level, the condemned sinner of 1.18—3.20 is promised that there is 'no condemnation' for those who are 'in the Messiah', because the condemnation of sin has already taken place in him.

There is no space left to reflect further on verse 4. It belongs, in any case, closely with the verses that follow, to which we now turn. But stay for a moment with the opening verses of chapter 8. You might even want to learn them by heart. You will seldom come upon a fuller or more exact statement of what God achieved in Jesus the Messiah, his son. Like someone in the desert discovering a small spring emerging from a huge cavern of water, there is enough here to live on for quite some time.

ROMANS 8.5–11

The Work of the Spirit

[5]Look at it like this. People whose lives are determined by human flesh focus their minds on matters to do with the flesh, but people whose lives are determined by the spirit focus their minds on matters to do with the spirit. [6]Focus on flesh, and you'll die; but focus on the spirit, and you'll have life, and peace. [7]The mind focused on the flesh, you see, is hostile to God. It doesn't submit to God's law; in fact, it can't. [8]Those who are determined by the flesh can't please God.

[9]But you're not people of flesh; you're people of the spirit (if indeed God's spirit lives within you; note that anyone who doesn't have the spirit of the Messiah doesn't belong to him). [10]But if the Messiah is in you, the body is indeed dead because of sin, but the spirit is life because of covenant faithfulness. [11]So, then, if the spirit of the one who raised Jesus from the dead lives within you, the one who raised the Messiah from the dead will give life to your mortal bodies, too, through his spirit who lives within you.

Imagine rummaging around in an old attic and coming upon what looks like a standard lamp. It has a very strange type of bulb, but an elegant stem; and the shade, though a bit dusty, is quite attractive. You bring it down into the house and consider it. If you didn't know very much about the history of lamps, you might even try attaching it to the electric mains. If you did, you would probably get a shock, literally and metaphorically.

This lamp isn't designed to run on electricity. It is the old type; it was made for gas.

An unlikely tale, perhaps. But it highlights the point Paul is making here, a point often missed when people read quickly through Romans. Remember, he is still talking about the Jewish **law** and the fact that it couldn't give the **life** it promised – and the fact, now, that God has done what the law could not do, with the result (verse 4) that 'the right and proper verdict of the law is fulfilled in us, as we live not according to the flesh but according to the **spirit**'. This is what Paul is now explaining in more detail, and taking forward to its proper conclusion.

The point is the same as in 7.14: human beings in their natural state, faced with God's law, are about as much use as a gas lamp plugged into the electric supply. 'I am made of flesh,' said Paul, 'sold under sin', whereas the law is 'spiritual'. Now we see what he has in mind: if the law is to give the life it promised (7.10), it's no good running it through the wrong sort of appliance. You'll only get an explosion – which is what 7.14–25 is about. It must be run through an appliance of the right sort, one designed to work in the same mode. In other words, it must be applied to someone whose very being is no longer 'fleshly' in the sense Paul means it in these chapters, but 'spiritual'.

But what do 'fleshly' and 'spiritual' mean? The first term, particularly, is so problematic that it would be nice (as I have tried to do with some other technical language) to avoid it altogether, but I have found that doing so produces even worse tangles. Better to learn, once and for all, that when Paul uses the word 'flesh' and other similar words he does *not* intend us simply to think of the 'physical' world, in our normal sense, as opposed to the 'non-physical'. He has other language for that. The word we translate, here and elsewhere, as 'flesh' refers to people or things who share the corruptibility and mortality of the world, and, often enough and certainly here, the rebellion of the world. 'Flesh' is a negative term. For Paul as a Jew the created order, the physical world, was good in itself. Only its wrong use, and its corruption and defacing, are bad. 'Flesh' highlights that wrong use, that corruption and decay.

'Spirit', by contrast, usually refers to God's own spirit, the **holy spirit**. Sometimes, as in the passage which follows, Paul refers to the human spirit, the inner reality of someone's life. But the first meaning is the important one here. Paul is taking the categories of Adam-humanity and **Messiah**-humanity, the two categories he has been developing ever since chapter 5, and is painting in yet one more colour. This time he will be able to show that, seen in this light, God has indeed done what the law wanted to do but could not – in other words, to give life.

This process is already under way in daily Christian living. You can tell the difference between those who are concerned with 'flesh' and those concerned with the 'spirit': what is their mind focused on? What are they thinking about most or all of the time? This is where we can see that 'flesh' means both more and less than 'the physical world': someone who is proud, or jealous, or slanderous is certainly concentrating on the 'flesh' in Paul's sense, even though the attitudes, and the subject-matter they focus on, may be abstract (non-physical) rather than concrete. But to live like that, as we saw already in chapter 1, is to court and invite death itself, whereas to focus on the spirit is to have life (the main point here) and peace (recalling 5.1). Paul explains in verses 7 and 8, looking back once more to 7.14: the mind characterized by 'flesh' is bound to be not only hostile to God but incapable of submitting to the law or pleasing God. Paul implies that the mind characterized by the spirit does in fact submit to, and fulfil, God's law.

What does this mean? Again, tantalizingly, he doesn't say precisely. We can see the end of the argument: those who have the spirit dwelling in them will be raised from the dead (that is, they will be given the life which the law promised). But not until 10.5–9 does he spell out the way in which he understands Christian **faith** itself as a fulfilment of the law; and not until 13.8–10 does he explain that those who obey the law of love are in fact fulfilling the moral commands of the **Torah**. In a tight argument like this, he is forced to presuppose all kinds of things, to hint rather than to spell out, in order to keep the forward movement going.

Where that forward movement takes us is to the promise of **resurrection**, the promise that we shall eventually be rescued, 'saved', from the corruption and decay of death itself. This will be the moment of final vindication, when God does something which will say, more loudly than any words could do, 'Here are my people,' and indeed, as we see later in the chapter, 'Here is my good creation.' Notice how Paul can alternate between the Messiah and the spirit: 'the spirit is in you,' he says, but then, 'the Messiah is in you' (compare Galatians 2.20; Colossians 1.27). Notice, too, how careful he is with the words that refer to Jesus. When God raised *Jesus* (the individual human being) from the dead, he raised the *Messiah*, the one who represents his people, and who therefore guarantees to that people that what happened to the *Messiah* will happen to them as well.

The spirit is thus the means by which one of the most important questions left over from the first section of the letter is finally answered. How can God declare in the present that those who believe the **gospel** are 'in the right', anticipating correctly the verdict of the last day? Paul's answer emerges here. The spirit works in the hearts of believers, to generate faith itself through the preaching of the gospel, then to generate the kind of life described in the second half of verses 4, 5 and 6, and then to work powerfully the other side of death to give new bodily life. That is why, ultimately, there is 'no condemnation' for those who are in the Messiah. That is why their future verdict, 'in the right', 'within the covenant', 'sins forgiven' can be brought forward into the present. 'The spirit is life because of **covenant** faithfulness' (verse 10) – God's covenant faithfulness, and perhaps theirs as well.

There is yet another dimension to this powerful paragraph. In Jewish thought, the living God who was over and above his creation was also mysteriously present within creation. Paul inherited a rich tradition of ways to refer to this presence: God's wisdom, God's spirit, God's glory (particularly as dwelling in the **Temple**), God's **word**, and of course God's law. We might even include God's son in this list, in view of the exalted things said about the coming king in 2 Samuel 7, Psalm 2 and elsewhere. What Paul has done in this passage is to draw on precisely these modes of speaking about divine activity to describe God's rescue operation for Israel and the world. God has fulfilled the law by sending the son, as Wisdom had been sent into the world according to some traditions. As a result, God's spirit now dwells in the hearts of his people, as the glory of God had dwelt in the Temple. Paul has not developed a regular formula for speaking about God from a Christian point of view. But he already possessed all the elements that would later be known as trinitarian theology.

A genuine theology will always be alive with faith and hope. This is no mere theoretical construction for the sake of tidying up a metaphysical scheme. Romans 8.1–11 carries the power of the gospel in every breath. If the church could hoist its sails and catch this wind, there is no knowing what might happen.

ROMANS 8.12–17

Children of God, Led by the Spirit

¹²So then, my dear family, we are in debt – but not to human flesh, to live our life in that way. ¹³If you live in accordance with the flesh, you will die; but if, by the spirit, you put to death the deeds of the body, you will live.

¹⁴All who are led by the spirit of God, you see, are God's children. ¹⁵You didn't receive a spirit of slavery, did you, to go back again into a state of fear? No: you received the spirit of sonship, in whom we call out 'Abba, father!' ¹⁶When that happens, it is the spirit itself testifying along with our spirit that we are God's children. ¹⁷And if we're children, we are also heirs:

heirs of God, and fellow heirs with the Messiah, as long as we suffer with him so that we may also be glorified with him.

Debt is one of the great problems of today's world.

When I was younger, banks didn't allow many people to run into debt. Credit cards hadn't been invented. Student loans were not even thought of. Of course, people still got into debt, but the controls were much tighter, and most people did their best to live within their income.

Today, all that has changed, and as far as I can see it's changed for the worse. Millions of people in the Western world live way beyond their means, taking out more and more loans and overdrafts, and getting more and more pieces of plastic, which then in turn run up even more interest and other charges.

Meanwhile, the Western world has set up a global economic system which apparently depends on keeping a large number of entire countries in massive and unpayable debt. Despite campaigns to increase public awareness of the problem, it still goes on. And it gets worse.

One of the most terrible things about debt is that it dominates your mind. Whatever else you might be going to think of, or plan or hope for, the fact that you're in debt determines the way you see the world.

So why does Paul begin this dramatic paragraph by saying we're in debt?

It seems to be another case of Paul starting something off and then getting sidetracked before he returns to finish the train of thought. From the previous paragraph, we might expect that he would tell us we should live our lives out of gratitude to the God who planned and accomplished our entire salvation. And so he will, beginning by telling us that we are in debt, meaning to go on to speak of the promised inheritance which we will share with the **Messiah** himself. He is God's unique son; we are God's adopted sons and daughters. That, it seems, is where Paul initially wanted this paragraph to go.

But as soon as he began it he found he had to underline the negative point already made in verses 5–8. We are *not* in debt to 'the flesh' (something he stresses again in 13.14); it has done us no favours, and we owe it none in return. If we try to live that way, we are simply inviting death, not (once more) as an arbitrary punishment but as the direct consequence. Instead, we are called to a life of saying 'No' to all kinds of things that our physical bodies tell us they want: here and in Colossians 3.9 Paul refers to this saying 'No' as a kind of 'putting to death'. This is bound to be hard and painful, but it must be done. A Christian life that does not involve putting to death that which drags us down into the world of the 'flesh' is not worthy of the name.

Paul's further explanation of all this takes him into territory we have mentioned before, but which we must now make more explicit. This is the point at which he begins to echo passages in the Old Testament which speak of the children of Israel travelling through the wilderness towards the promised land.

The Israelites were led by God himself, going with them in the pillar of cloud by day and the pillar of fire by night. At various times they wanted to give up and go back to Egypt, where they had been in slavery; but they clung on, despite rebellion, idolatry and a host of other follies. At the back of it all was the summons near the start of the book of Exodus: 'Israel is my son, my firstborn; let my people go so that they can serve me!' (Exodus 4.22, picked up in Hosea 11.1). The point of it all was that they would arrive at last in the land which was to be given them as an inheritance.

When we read Romans 8 with this theme in mind, we can hardly miss the echoes – though the way they appear is very revealing. The wilderness, the desert land, seems to be the world in which the lure of 'flesh' remains strong, and must be resisted. Instead of the pillars of cloud and fire, Christians are given the **spirit** as the personal presence of the living God (wouldn't it be fine if all Christians were as much in awe of the fact of the

145

spirit's dwelling in and with them as the Israelites learned to be with the presence of God in cloud and fire). Christians will often be tempted to give up the struggle and go back to Egypt, to the place of slavery. Even though they have left it behind, as Paul makes clear in 6.15–19, there are many times when it would seem so much easier to be enslaved to sin again – no more battles, no more sense of an uphill struggle . . . and no more inheritance to look forward to, no living presence of God, no sense of companionship with Jesus himself. 'You didn't receive a spirit of slavery, did you, to go back again into a state of fear?' No, of course not. Don't be surprised if the way is hard and stony. It's always like that when you go from Egypt to Canaan.

In particular, the Christian discovers a new identity, picking up Israel's vocation in the Old Testament: adoption. When the **holy spirit** comes to dwell in a person's heart, the first sign is that they recognize God as father; this, I think, is part of what Paul meant in 5.5 when he spoke of a love for God being poured out in our hearts by the holy spirit. The cry 'Abba, father' uses the old Aramaic word which Jesus himself had used for God (Mark 14.36). Paul refers to the same cry in Galatians 4.5–6, where again there are powerful echoes of the **Exodus** story. This time he interprets what is going on in terms of the coming together of the holy spirit with our own spirit.

This is a delicate matter to describe. It is, however, a common Christian experience that while many of the thoughts in our mind seem to come from the ordinary flow of consciousness within us, sometimes we find other thoughts, which seem to come from somewhere else, hinting gently but powerfully at God's love, at our calling to holiness, at particular tasks to which we must give energy and attention. A key part of Christian discipleship is to recognize that voice, and to nurture the facility of listening to it. It is, or may well be, the voice of God's own spirit. And one of the primary things the spirit says, with which we find our own spirit in full agreement, is that we are indeed God's children, God's adopted sons and daughters. This remains an important theme in the following discussion (see 8.29).

But the key move is yet to come. The children of Israel were promised an inheritance, namely, the land of Canaan. This was already widened dramatically in God's promise to the coming Messiah in Psalm 2.8: 'I will give you the nations as your inheritance, and the uttermost parts of the earth as your possession.' This in turn is projected back on to the promise to Abraham, as we saw in 4.13: the promise to Abraham and his family, declares Paul, is that they should inherit the *world*. Now, in the passage we are about to reach, we see what this means in fully Christian terms. It means that the whole world, the entire creation, is going to be made over to the Messiah and his people, and with their eventual vindication and **resurrection** that entire creation will itself be set free from corruption and decay.

This gives us a hint of what 'glorification' (already promised in 5.2) actually means. It doesn't mean that we shall shine like human electric light bulbs (though there are promises like that too, for instance in Daniel 12.3 and Matthew 13.43). It means that we will share the Messiah's glorious rule over the world. That is what Paul said already in 5.17. Here he has arrived at the same point by another road.

This, then, is why we are 'debtors'. We are debtors to the God who loved us, who has saved us, and who is leading us home to the land we have been promised, the eventual new creation. Inheriting that, we shall for ever be in God's debt, and should recognize that already and live accordingly. Debtors, after all, are under an obligation. Some Christians speak and live as if everything simply comes to us from God while we sit still and merely receive it. But God's gift and call to us are not for ourselves alone, but for the purpose of working through us to bring about the transformation of the world. Some people get anxious about implying that we have to *do* anything ourselves as Christians at any stage of the process, in case such action appears to compromise the free grace by which we are saved. But Paul declares that we are debtors. We have to live in a particular way, a way which anticipates the 'glory', the rule over creation, which we will eventually share with the Messiah. And that, in the present, will mean suffering.

ROMANS 8.18–25

Creation Renewed and Patient Hope

[18]This is how I work it out. The sufferings we go through in the present time are not worth putting in the scale alongside the glory that is going to be unveiled for us. [19]Yes: creation itself is on tiptoe with expectation, eagerly awaiting the moment when God's children will be revealed. [20]Creation, you see, was subjected to pointless futility, not of its own volition, but because of the one who placed it in this subjection, in the hope [21]that creation itself would be freed from its slavery to decay, to enjoy the freedom that comes when God's children are glorified.

[22]Let me explain. We know that the entire creation is groaning together, and going through labour pains together, up until the present time. [23]Not only so: we too, we who have the first fruits of the spirit's life within us, are groaning within ourselves, as we eagerly await our adoption, the redemption of our body. [24]We were saved, you see, in hope. But hope isn't hope if you can see it! Who hopes for what they can see? [25]But if we hope for what we don't see, we wait for it eagerly – but also patiently.

I walked through the wood several times before I realized what the signpost meant.

The wood was thick, with paths leading this way and that. I knew some of them quite well, and had my favourites among them. There was the one that led round by the lake, another that took you to a splendid little clearing where you would usually see rabbits and squirrels. There was another one that led past some ancient oak trees, of the sort that I imagine would have witnessed battles hundreds of years ago.

But there was another path which I had never taken. It looked a bit overgrown and I couldn't see where it would go. Because on most of my walks I'm in a hurry to get exercise and then get back to work, I never bothered with it. Nor did I give a second thought to a small post which stood, almost hidden behind bushes, just beside the start of the path. It had what looked like the letter V at the top, a foot or two from the ground. For all I knew, it was just a mark cut in the wood. It didn't necessarily mean anything.

Until one day I came past the place, and someone had cleared the bushes enough to reveal three other letters, and an arrow pointing along the path. The other letters, downwards from the V, were I, E and W. A *view*? What sort of a view? Intrigued, I took the path for the first time.

To begin with, it was as I'd expected: overgrown (I obviously wasn't the only one who'd ignored it), with brambles and thorns in the way. It was muddy underfoot, as well; I wished I'd had my thicker boots on. But then it turned sharply through the trees and began to climb quite steeply. I was out of breath in a few minutes, but after a brief pause I kept going, getting more excited. Suddenly, instead of thick trees all around me, I saw clear sky emerging. Then I was out of the trees and onto a slab of rock. I scrambled up it and stood there calling myself names for never finding the spot before.

It was indeed a view. I was looking down not only on the whole large wood but also on the little town beyond it. I could see other hills in the distance, and smoke rising from villages in between. Half the county seemed to lie there before me. And I might never have known.

Romans 8.18–25 is like that view. From this point we can see, in astonishing clarity, the whole plan of salvation for all of God's creation. Once you've glimpsed this view, you will never forget it. And yet most readers of Romans, for many years and in many traditions, have hurried on by. They have been busy with theories of individual **justification** and salvation. They have been eager for moral lessons, for a fresh experience of the **spirit** (or a fresh theology to back up the experience they've had). They have been on their way to the great questions about Israel and the **Gentiles**, which do indeed preoccupy a good deal of Romans, not least the next few chapters.

And the signpost which might have told them to turn this way and walk up this path has been covered in bushes and brambles. The language of creation on tiptoe with expectation is not what they expect. The strange idea of God subjecting creation to futility and slavery, and of creation then being rescued, simply isn't what people wanted to hear, or knew how to interpret when they did. The old King James translation probably didn't help either, by saying 'creature' when today's word would be 'creation', giving the average reader the puzzle of wondering which 'creature' Paul was talking about. So the path to the viewpoint has been covered over with thorns and thistles. 'Strange apocalyptic ideas', people have said, and hurried on to safer ground. But this is the place to visit. From the top of this hill you can see for ever.

After all, if you were Paul, writing a carefully crafted letter like Romans, would you build up all this time to such a pitch of excitement and then, with the end of this train of thought nearly in sight, allow yourself to ramble on about irrelevancies for a couple of paragraphs? Of course not. This passage is near the climax of the chapter which is itself the climax of the letter so far. Of course it's central. Of course it's vital to his thinking. The fact that he doesn't say anything quite like this elsewhere is neither here nor there. A good deal of Romans is like that.

He begins where the previous paragraph left off, with the promise that the present suffering, though often intense, will be far outweighed by 'the glory that is going to be unveiled for us'. Note, unveiled *for us*. Not 'in us', as though glorification were after all simply us looking pleased with ourselves. Not 'to us', as though we were going to be spectators of 'glory', like people watching a fireworks display. The point of 'glory' is that it means glorious, sovereign rule, sharing the **Messiah**'s saving rule over the whole world. And that is what the whole creation is waiting for. It is waiting for us, for you and me, for all God's children, to be revealed. Then, at last, creation will see its true rulers, and will know that the time has come for it to be rescued from corruption.

To understand this, we need to grasp the big biblical story of creation. When we look at the world of creation as it is in the present, we see a world in the same condition as the children of Israel were in when they were enslaved in Egypt. Just as God allowed the Israelites to go down into Egypt, so that in bringing them out he could define them for ever as the freedom-from-slavery people, so God has allowed creation to be subjected to its present round of summer and winter, growth and decay, birth and death. It's beautiful, yes, but it always ends in tears or at least a shrug of the shoulders. If you happen to live at the sharp end of the corruption of creation – on an earthquake fault line, for instance, or by an active volcano – you may sense the awe of that futile power. Creation can sometimes appear like a caged buffalo: all that energy, and it's not achieving anything. And, thinking of wild animals, what about that promise of the wolf and the lamb lying down together? Is that just a dream?

No, says Paul, it isn't a dream. It's a promise. All these things are signs that the world as it is, though still God's good creation, and pregnant with his power and glory (1.20), is not at present the way it should be. God's '**covenant** faithfulness' was always about his commitment that, through the promises to Abraham, he would one day put the whole world to rights. Now at last we see what this meant. The human race was put in charge of creation (as so often, Paul has Genesis 1—3 not far from his mind). When humans rebelled and worshipped parts of creation instead of God himself (1.21–23), creation fell into disrepair. God allowed this state of slavery to continue, not because the creation wanted to be like that but because he was determined eventually to put the world back to rights according to the original plan (just as, when Israel let him down, he didn't change the plan, but sent at last a faithful Israelite). The plan had called for human beings to take their place under God and over the world, worshipping the creator and exercising glorious stewardship over the world. The creation isn't waiting to *share* the freedom of God's children, as some translations imply. It is waiting to benefit wonderfully when God's children are glorified. It is waiting – on tiptoe with expectation, in fact – for the particular freedom it will enjoy when God gives to his children that glory, that wise rule and stewardship, which was always intended for those who bear God's glorious image.

This perspective on the whole created order has all kinds of implications, from the way we think about the ultimate future for the world and ourselves (the end of the story is not a disembodied 'heaven' but a whole new world) to our present anticipation of that final responsibility for God's world. This is a positive, world-affirming view, without any of the risks associated with pantheism (idolatry, and the lack of any critique of evil). There are many avenues here we might like to explore.

But Paul moves at once to consider the present position of God's children in the light of this future. We are, he says, longing for the time when we ourselves will be fully and finally redeemed, when, that is, we will receive our promised **resurrection** bodies. We groan and sigh, if we know what we are about, as we experience the tension between the glorious promise and the present reality. This tension is encapsulated in the fact that the spirit is already at work within us, but has not yet completed the task of our full renewal. We have the 'first fruits' of the spirit's **life**; Paul uses the harvesting image of early sheaves offered to God as the sign of a great crop still to come. We are left with a striking analysis of Christian hope, hope that, like **faith**, is not seen (or it wouldn't be hope at all), but hope that is certain none the less. Groaning and waiting, eager but patient: that is the characteristic Christian stance.

Paul's larger picture locates this groaning on the map of all creation. At the centre of this remarkable passage is one of his most vivid images of hope: that of birth-pangs. The whole creation is in labour, longing for God's new world to be born. The church is called to share that pain and that hope. The church is not to be apart from the pain of the world; it is to be in prayer at precisely the place where the world is in pain. That is part of our calling, our high but strange role within God's purposes for new creation.

ROMANS 8.26–30
Prayer, Sonship and the Sovereignty of God

26In the same way, too, the spirit comes alongside and helps us in our weakness. We don't know what to pray for as we ought to; but that same spirit pleads on our behalf, with groanings too deep for words. 27And the Searcher of Hearts knows what the spirit is thinking, because the spirit pleads for God's people according to God's will.

28We know, in fact, that God works all things together for good to those who love him, who are called according to his purpose. 29Those he foreknew, you see, he also marked out in advance to be shaped according to the model of the image of his son, so that he might be the firstborn of a large family. 30And those he marked out in advance, he also called; those he called, he also justified; those he justified, he also glorified.

How many names can you think of for God? It may sound an odd question. God's proper name in the Old Testament is of course YHWH; but he is referred to in a great many other ways as well, such as 'the Almighty', the Holy One of Israel', or 'YHWH of Hosts'. He is, of course, regularly called 'the God of Abraham', sometimes with Isaac and Jacob added as well. Other, stranger names appear fleetingly; Jacob, apparently, knows God as 'the Fear of his father Isaac' (Genesis 31.42, 53) – at least until he wrestles with God face to face in the next chapter.

It would be worth making a study of the various names, titles and descriptions of God scattered liberally around the New Testament as well. In John's **gospel**, Jesus regularly refers to God in terms of his own mission: 'the father who sent me'. Here in Romans itself, God has been referred to variously as 'the one who raised Jesus from the dead' (4.24; 8.11). Now, in this passage, we have an equally powerful but more mysterious title: 'the Searcher of Hearts'. This is a disturbing and exciting idea, and we ought to examine it a bit closer.

We have already been told that God will eventually judge all human secrets (2.16). Paul has insisted that God will reserve praise for the person who is a Jew 'in secret' as opposed to mere outward qualification (2.29). But verse 27 of the present passage goes a step further. The word 'searcher' comes from a root which suggests someone lighting a torch and going slowly round a large, dark room full of all sorts of things, looking for something in particular. Or perhaps he is searching in the dark, by listening. What is he wanting to find, and what happens when he finds it?

No doubt God, in searching the dark spaces of our hearts, comes across all sorts of things which we would just as soon remained hidden. But the thing he is wanting to find above all else, and which according to Paul he ought to find in all Christians, is the sound of the **spirit**'s groaning.

We saw in the last section that the world is in pain, groaning in the birth-pangs of new creation. We saw, too, that the church shares this pain, groaning in our longing for our own redeemed bodies, suffering in the tension between the 'already' of possessing the first fruits of the spirit and the 'not yet' of our present mortal existence. The church is not to be apart from the pain of the world; now we discover that God himself does not stand apart from the pain both of the world and of the church, but comes to dwell in the middle of it in the person and power of the spirit.

Paul's understanding of the spirit is new and striking at this point. At the very moment when we are struggling to pray, and have no idea even what to pray for, just at that point the spirit is most obviously at work. The spirit calls out of us not articulate speech – that would be a relief, and we are not yet ready for relief in this work of prayer – but a groaning which cannot at the moment come into words. This is prayer beyond prayer, diving down into the cold, dark depths beyond human sight or knowing.

But not beyond the Searcher of Hearts. As part of Paul's picture, not just of the world or the church, but of God, we discover that the transcendent creator is continually in communion with the spirit who dwells in the hearts of his people. God understands what the spirit is saying, even though we do not. God hears and answers the prayer which we only know as painful groanings, the tossings and turnings of an unquiet spirit standing before its maker with the pains and puzzles of the world heavy on its heart. There is a challenge here to every church, and every Christian: to be willing to shoulder the task of prayer of this kind, prayer in which we are caught up in the loving, groaning, redeeming dialogue between the father and the spirit.

This is, in fact, what our 'glorified' sovereignty over the world looks like in practice *in the **present age***. The challenge to suffer with the **Messiah** in order to be glorified with him means, to be sure, being ready for all kinds of physical suffering, persecution and the like (8.35–36). That is what often comes from worshipping the true God while the world is still out of joint. But, just as personal holiness is to be seen as taking responsibility in the present for that part of the created order most obviously under our own control, in anticipation of the day when we shall 'reign in life' over considerably larger spheres, so prayer, seen in the light of verses 26 and 27, can be understood as taking responsibility for that larger world itself, in advance of the new creation, and as sharing in the sufferings of the Messiah as we do so. To be sure, there are plenty of things in the world for which we can and must pray articulately. But there are plenty of others where all we can do is to be still in God's presence and allow the spirit to groan, and the Searcher of Hearts to search for that groaning and to recognize it as what it is: suffering according to the pattern of the Messiah.

Being conformed in this way to the image of God's son is, in fact, what God has purposed for us all along. Prayer of this kind is simply part of the 'conforming' process, as there appears in our hearts that love for God of which, as we saw at 5.5, the ancient Jewish 'Shema' prayer had spoken. When we are thus marked out as God's people, not outwardly but in the secret prayers and loves of our inmost being, we can be completely sure that God is in charge, that he can bring good out of whatever happens. Verse 28 is a much-loved promise for many who have learned by it to trust God in the many varied and often troubling circumstances of our lives. The world is still groaning, and we with it; but God is with us in this groaning, and will bring it out for good.

This belief broadens out into Paul's climactic statement, in verses 29 and 30, of God's purpose for all his children. As with Israel in the Old Testament, so Paul understands those who have now been brought into fellowship with and through his son to have been 'foreknown'. They did not choose God, but he chose them, in a mystery which Paul does not attempt to penetrate, either here or elsewhere. Instead, he concentrates on that which God planned and purposed for them: that they should be shaped into the pattern or model of Jesus, the true 'image of God', becoming thereby genuinely human as they join the family as younger brothers and sisters of the truly human one.

The last verse sets out the simple but profound steps by which God goes to work to call out those who, in his purpose, are now to share the image of his son, to be among those summoned to advance his work in the world. Those who were marked out for this task in the first place have been, mysteriously, 'called'; Paul uses 'call' as a technical term for what happens when the preaching of the gospel works powerfully in someone's life to bring them to **faith**, to urge them to **baptism**, and to flood their hearts with love for God by the spirit. When the gospel produces faith in this way, as we have seen, God declares the person to be indeed a true member of the family: the word for that is '**justification**'. And the purpose of it all, a purpose which is every bit as secure as those that have gone before, so much so that like the others it can be spoken of in the past tense, is that they may be 'glorified', sharing the Messiah's sovereign, redeeming rule over the whole creation. The whole passage seems designed to remind us both of the sovereignty of God and of the fact that this sovereignty is always exercised in love.

ROMANS 8.31–39

Nothing Shall Separate Us from God's Love

[31]What then shall we say to all this?
If God is for us, who is against us?
[32]God, after all, did not spare his own son; he gave him up for us all!
How then will he not, with him, freely give all things to us?
[33]Who will bring a charge against God's chosen ones?
It is God who declares them in the right.
[34]Who is going to condemn?
It is the Messiah, Jesus, who has died, or rather has been raised;
who is at God's right hand, and who also prays on our behalf!
[35]Who shall separate us from the Messiah's love?
Suffering, or hardship, or persecution, or famine, or nakedness, or danger, or sword? [36]As the Bible says,

Because of you we are being killed all day long
We are regarded as sheep destined for slaughter.

157

[37]No: in all these things we are completely victorious through the one who loved us. [38]I am persuaded, you see, that neither death nor life, nor angels nor rulers, nor the present, nor the future, nor powers, [39]nor height nor depth nor any other creature will be able to separate us from the love of God in King Jesus our Lord.

Terrible tales emerge from wars, terrorist action, and other violent scenes. Those held hostage in Lebanon in the 1980s tell of more than one occasion when they were taken off, blindfolded, and told they were going to die. A gun would be pressed against their heads, held there for an agonizing moment, and then, with a crude laugh or a kick, they were sent back to their cells. The sense of relief, coupled with the knowledge that it might happen for real the next day, is hard to imagine. Finally, when the hostages were released, it must have taken them months, if not years, before they could wake up in the morning and know that their enemies had gone, that nobody was going to threaten them any more.

Other tales resonate with this sense of surprising release. Jesus confronts the self-righteous men about to stone a woman taken in adultery (John 8.1–11). She has been kneeling or lying on the ground, waiting in terror for the first rock to smash into her, maiming her cruelly, most likely, long before the eventual release of death. Now she looks up. The men have all gone, shamed by Jesus' challenge to their own sinful lives. What, asks Jesus with wry humour, has no one condemned you?

Something of that same air of surprised relief pervades the closing section of this astonishing chapter. We look around to see who has condemned us, and discover that they've all gone. Four times the question is asked, and each time the implied answer is resounding. Who is against us? No one; God, after all, has given us his son and will give us all things with him. Who will bring a charge against us? No one; God himself has **justified** us, has already declared us to be in the right. Who will condemn us? No one; Jesus has died, been raised and exalted, and intercedes for us. Who shall separate us from his love? No one; this time there are many contenders that might try, but the note of victory sounds out. Nothing in all creation can separate us from the love of God in King Jesus.

That is the formal structure of the paragraph, and as its content suggests it is full of a sustained excitement, like a symphony entering its final moments and getting faster and faster towards the end, with phrases taken from earlier parts of the music being whirled around in triumph. The paragraph is, in fact, a summary of the whole theme of chapters 5–8, presented now not as a step-by-step argument, as it has been up to this point, but as a thrilling rhetorical statement. Look what God has done. Look what the **Messiah** has done, and is still doing even as we speak. Look around and see the many things that threaten to separate you from the powerful love which reaches out through the cross and **resurrection**, and learn that they are all beaten foes. Learn to dance and sing for joy to celebrate the victory of God. The end of Romans 8 deserves to be written in letters of fire on the living tablets of our hearts.

It also deserves to be pondered more slowly, and its implications thoroughly digested. The whole section from chapter 5 onwards has been an argument about *assurance*. This is often mocked: fancy thinking, we are told, that you can be *sure* of God's love and of your own salvation. How very arrogant! How very self-centred! But the sting of these sneers can be drawn (without even making the obvious point, that they may arise from envy). The claim in verse 31 that 'God is for us' sounds glib when we think of armies going to war and claiming divine protection for their side. It sounds very different when made by an **apostle** who has faced hardship, persecution, danger and death. As in 5.1–5 and 8.17, the claim that hope will not let us down can only be made as we are sharing the sufferings of the Messiah.

Granted that, the weight of the letter so far comes down

heavily on the meaning of **justification**: God has declared all those who believe in the **gospel** to be in the right, and no one will be able to overturn God's verdict. Justification by **faith** is after all the ground of assurance, not of justification itself. We are not justified by faith by believing in justification by faith; we are justified by faith by believing in the gospel, by believing (that is) in Jesus as the crucified and risen Lord of the world. When we understand justification, we gain, not justification itself, but assurance. The God who has called us in the gospel has declared that we are members of his family, and he will not let us go. This passage thus looks on to the final day of judgment, completing the large circle of meaning begun in chapter 2, and declares that on that final day God will reaffirm the verdict already issued on the basis of faith.

One of the answers reveals a dimension to the work of the Messiah not mentioned anywhere else in his letters (reminding us that there may have been many things Paul took for granted which he happens not to have written in letters that have come down to us). The present work of Jesus, following his death, resurrection and exaltation, consists in praying for his people at the father's right hand (verse 35; the same theme appears in Hebrews 7.25 and 9.24, and in 1 John 2.1, and is probably in mind in Acts 7.55). This thought is a great comfort, especially when the going is tough, as it often was for Paul and as it often will be for those who follow and live by his gospel.

As so often in his writings in general and in Romans in particular, Paul draws on the Bible as his basic resource. He alludes in verse 32 to the story of Abraham giving up Isaac, his only son, a near-**sacrifice** which many Jews regarded as a key moment in the launching of the **covenant**. God, says Paul, has done what Abraham did, only much, much more. He echoes in verses 33 and 34 one of the 'Servant Songs' from Isaiah (50.4–9); from one point of view he sees Jesus himself as the 'Servant', but from another he regards the servant role as one which Jesus shares with his followers, himself included, as they live out his gospel in the world.

Then, in verse 36, he quotes Psalm 44.22, a psalm of complaint to God in the midst of suffering. The suffering, in the Psalm, has not come about because of Israel's infidelity. It has come about despite the fact that Israel has been faithful. Here, as in the 'Servant' passages in Isaiah, we find a truth deeply embedded in Judaism, and drawn on by several early Christians and arguably by Jesus himself: that God will save his people, not *despite* their sufferings but through and even because of them. Somehow, as in Colossians 1.24, the sufferings of God's people are taken up into God's purposes, not in order to add to the unique achievement of the Messiah (verse 34) but in order to live it out in the world so that his love might extend yet further. Those who believe this can be sure that 'in all these things we are completely victorious through the one who loved us.'

It is that love, finally, that comes back again and again, not as an afterthought but as the underlying theme of the entire section. We cast our minds back to 5.1–11, where the love of God was demonstrated in the death of Jesus, and we realize that we have come full circle. John Donne, indeed, likened the love of God to a circle, seeing that it is endless. It rules victoriously over death and **life** alike, over powers in **heaven** and on earth. And since it is love's nature to bind the beloved to itself, Paul is convinced, and after eight chapters of Romans he might expect that we would be as well, that 'nothing in all creation can separate us from the love of God in King Jesus our Lord.'

GLOSSARY

age to come, *see* **present age**

apostle, disciple, the Twelve

'Apostle' means 'one who is sent'. It could be used of an ambassador or official delegate. In the New Testament it is sometimes used specifically of Jesus' inner circle of twelve; but Paul sees not only himself but several others outside the Twelve as 'apostles', the criterion being whether the person had personally seen the risen Jesus. Jesus' own choice of twelve close associates symbolized his plan to renew God's people, Israel; after the death of Judas Iscariot (Matthew 27.5; Acts 1.18) Matthias was chosen by lot to take his place, preserving the symbolic meaning. During Jesus' lifetime they, and many other followers, were seen as his 'disciples', which means 'pupils' or 'apprentices'.

baptism

Literally, 'plunging' people into water. From within a wider Jewish tradition of ritual washings and bathings, **John the Baptist** undertook a vocation of baptizing people in the Jordan, not as one ritual among others but as a unique moment of **repentance**, preparing them for the coming of the **kingdom of God**. Jesus himself was baptized by John, identifying himself with this renewal movement and developing it in his own way. His followers in turn baptized others. After his **resurrection**, and the sending of the **holy spirit**, baptism became the normal sign and means of entry into the community of Jesus' people. As early as Paul it was aligned both with the **Exodus** from Egypt (1 Corinthians 10.2) and with Jesus' death and resurrection (Romans 6.2–11).

Christ, *see* **Messiah**

circumcision, circumcised

The cutting off of the foreskin. Male circumcision was a major mark of identity for Jews, following its initial commandment to Abraham (Genesis 17), reinforced by Joshua (Joshua 5.2–9). Other peoples, e.g. the Egyptians, also circumcised male children. A line of thought from Deuteronomy (e.g. 30.6), through Jeremiah (e.g. 31.33), to the **Dead Sea Scrolls** and the New Testament (e.g. Romans 2.29) speaks of 'circumcision of the heart' as God's real desire, by which one may become inwardly what the male Jew is outwardly, that is, marked out as part of God's people. At periods of Jewish assimilation into the surrounding culture, some Jews tried to remove the marks of circumcision (e.g. 1 Maccabees 1.11–15).

covenant

At the heart of Jewish belief is the conviction that the one God, YHWH, who had made the whole world, had called Abraham and his family to belong to him in a special way. The promises God made to Abraham and his family, and the requirements that were laid on them as a result, came to be seen in terms either of the agreement that a king would make with a subject people, or sometimes of the marriage bond between husband and wife. One regular way of describing this relationship was 'covenant', which can thus include both promise and **law**. The covenant was renewed at Mount Sinai with the giving of the **Torah**; in Deuteronomy before the entry to the promised land; and, in a more focused way, with **David** (e.g. Psalm 89). Jeremiah 31 promised that after the punishment of **exile** God would make a 'new covenant' with his people, forgiving them and binding them to him more intimately. Jesus believed that this was coming true through his **kingdom** proclamation and his death and **resurrection**. The early Christians developed these ideas in various ways, believing that in Jesus the promises had at last been fulfilled.

David, *see* son of David

Dead Sea Scrolls

A collection of texts, some in remarkably good repair, some extremely fragmentary, found in the late 1940s around Qumran (near the northeast corner of the Dead Sea), and virtually all now edited, translated and in the public domain. They formed all or part of the library of a strict monastic group, most likely Essenes, founded in the mid-second century BC and lasting until the Jewish–Roman war of 66–70. The scrolls include the earliest existing manuscripts of the Hebrew and Aramaic scriptures, and several other important documents of community regulations, scriptural exegesis, hymns, wisdom writings, and other literature. They shed a flood of light on one small segment within the Judaism of Jesus' day, helping us to understand how some Jews at least were thinking, praying and reading scripture. Despite attempts to prove the contrary, they make no reference to **John the Baptist**, Jesus, Paul, James or early Christianity in general.

disciple, *see* **apostle**

Essenes, *see* **Dead Sea Scrolls**

eternal life, *see* **present age**

eucharist

The meal in which the earliest Christians, and Christians ever since, obeyed Jesus' command to 'do this in remembrance of him' at the Last Supper (Luke 22.19; 1 Corinthians 11.23–26). The word 'eucharist' itself comes from the Greek for 'thanksgiving'; it means, basically, 'the thank-you meal', and looks back to the many times when Jesus took bread, gave thanks for it, broke it, and gave it to people (e.g. Luke 24.30; John 6.11). Other early phrases for the same meal are 'the Lord's supper' (1 Corinthians 11.20) and 'the breaking of bread' (Acts 2.42). Later it came to be called 'the Mass' (from the Latin word at the end of the service, meaning 'sent out') and 'Holy Communion' (Paul speaks of 'sharing' or 'communion' in the body and blood of Christ). Later theological controversies about the precise meaning of the various actions and elements of the meal should not obscure its centrality in earliest Christian living and its continuing vital importance today.

exile

Deuteronomy (29—30) warned that if Israel disobeyed YHWH, he would send his people into exile, but that if they then repented he would bring them back. When the Babylonians sacked Jerusalem and took the people into exile, prophets such as Jeremiah interpreted this as the fulfilment of this prophecy, and made further promises about how long exile would last (70 years, according to Jeremiah 25.12; 29.10). Sure enough, exiles began to return in the late sixth century (Ezra 1.1). However, the post-exilic period was largely a disappointment, since the people were still enslaved to foreigners (Nehemiah 9.36); and at the height of persecution by the Syrians, Daniel 9.2, 24 spoke of the 'real' exile lasting not for 70 years but for 70 *weeks* of years, i.e. 490 years. Longing for the real 'return from exile', when the prophecies of Isaiah, Jeremiah, etc. would be fulfilled, and redemption from pagan oppression accomplished, continued to characterize many Jewish movements, and was a major theme in Jesus' proclamation and his summons to **repentance**.

Exodus

The Exodus from Egypt took place, according to the book of that name, under the leadership of Moses, after long years in which the Israelites had been enslaved there. (According to Genesis 15.13f., this was itself part of God's covenanted promise to Abraham.) It demon-strated, to them and to Pharaoh, King of Egypt, that Israel was God's special child (Exodus 4.22). They then wandered through the Sinai wilderness for 40 years, led by God in a pillar of cloud and fire; early on in this time they were given the **Torah** on Mount Sinai itself. Finally, after the death of Moses and under the leadership of Joshua, they crossed the Jordan and entered, and eventually conquered, the promised land of Canaan. This event, commemorated annually in Passover and other Jewish festivals, gave the Israelites not only a powerful memory of what had made them a people, but also a particular shape and content to their faith in YHWH as not only creator but also redeemer; and in subsequent enslavements, particularly the **exile**, they looked for a further redemption which would be, in effect, a new Exodus. Probably no other past event so dominated the imagination of first-century Jews; among them the early Christians, following the lead of Jesus himself, continually referred back to the Exodus to give meaning and shape to their own critical events, most particularly Jesus' death and **resurrection**.

faith

Faith in the New Testament covers a wide area of human trust and trustworthiness, merging into love at one end of the scale and loyalty at the other. Within Jewish and Christian thinking faith in God also includes *belief*, accepting certain things as true about God, and what he has done in the world (e.g. bringing Israel out of Egypt; raising Jesus from the dead). For Jesus, 'faith' often seems to mean 'recognizing that God is decisively at work to bring the **kingdom** through Jesus'. For Paul, 'faith' is both the specific belief that Jesus is Lord and that God raised him from the dead (Romans 10.9) and the response of grateful human love to sovereign divine love (Galatians 2.20). This faith is, for Paul, the solitary badge of membership in God's people in **Christ**, marking them out in a way that **Torah**, and the works it prescribes, can never do.

Gehenna, hell

Gehenna is, literally, the valley of Hinnom, on the south-west slopes of Jerusalem. From ancient times it was used as a garbage dump, smouldering with a continual fire. Already by the time of Jesus some Jews used it as an image for the place of punishment after death. Jesus' own usage blends the two meanings in his warnings both to Jerusalem itself (unless it repents, the whole city will become a smouldering heap of garbage) and to people in general (to beware of God's final judgment).

Gentiles

The Jews divided the world into Jews and non-Jews. The Hebrew word for non-Jews, *goyim*, carries overtones both of family identity (i.e., not of Jewish ancestry) and of worship (i.e., of idols, not of the one true God YHWH). Though many Jews established good relations with Gentiles, not least in the Jewish Diaspora (the dispersion of Jews away from Palestine), officially there were taboos against contact such as intermarriage. In the New Testament the Greek word *ethne*, 'nations', carries the same meanings as *goyim*. Part of Paul's overmastering agenda was to insist that Gentiles who believed in Jesus had full rights in the Christian community alongside believing Jews, without having to become **circumcised**.

good news, gospel, message, word

The idea of 'good news', for which an older English word is 'gospel', had two principal meanings for first-century Jews. First, with roots in Isaiah, it meant the news of YHWH's long-awaited victory over evil and rescue of his people. Second, it was used in the Roman world of the accession, or birthday, or the emperor. Since for Jesus and Paul the announcement of God's inbreaking **kingdom** was both the fulfilment of prophecy and a challenge to the world's present rulers, 'gospel' became an important shorthand for both the message of Jesus himself, and the apostolic message about him. Paul saw this message as itself the vehicle of God's saving power (Romans 1.16; 1 Thessalonians 2.13).

The four canonical 'gospels' tell the story of Jesus in such a way as to bring out both these aspects (unlike some other so-called 'gospels' circulated in the second and subsequent centuries, which tended both to cut off the scriptural and Jewish roots of Jesus' achievement and to inculcate a private spirituality rather than confrontation with the world's rulers). Since in Isaiah this creative, life-giving good news was seen as God's own powerful word (40.8; 55.11), the early Christians could use 'word' or 'message' as another shorthand for the basic Christian proclamation.

gospel, *see* **good news**

heaven

Heaven is God's dimension of the created order (Genesis 1.1; Psalm 115.16; Matthew 6.9), whereas 'earth' is the world of space, time and matter that we know. 'Heaven' thus sometimes stands, reverentially, for 'God' (as in Matthew's regular '**kingdom** of heaven'). Normally hidden from human sight, heaven is occasionally revealed or unveiled so that people can see God's dimension of ordinary life (e.g. 2 Kings 6.17; Revelation 1, 4—5). Heaven in the New Testament is thus not usually seen as the place where God's people go after death; at the end the New Jerusalem descends *from* heaven *to* earth, joining the two dimensions for ever. 'Entering the kingdom of heaven' does not mean 'going to heaven after death', but belonging in the present to the people who steer their earthly course by the standards and purposes of heaven (cf. the Lord's Prayer: 'on earth as in heaven', Matthew 6. 10) and who are assured of membership in the **age to come**.

hell, *see* **Gehenna**

holy spirit

In Genesis 1.2, the spirit is God's presence and power *within* creation, without God being identified with creation. The same spirit entered people, notably the prophets, enabling them to speak and act for God. At his **baptism** by **John the Baptist**, Jesus was specially equipped with the spirit, resulting in his remarkable public career (Acts 10.38). After his **resurrection**, his followers were themselves filled (Acts 2) by the same spirit, now identified as Jesus' own spirit: the creator God was acting afresh, remaking the world and them too. The spirit enabled them to live out a holiness which the **Torah** could not, producing 'fruit' in their lives, giving them 'gifts' with which to serve God, the world, and the church, and assuring them of future resurrection (Romans 8; Galatians 4—5; 1 Corinthians 12—14). From very early in Christianity (e.g. Galatians 4.1–7), the spirit became part of the new revolutionary definition of God himself: 'the one who sends the son and the spirit of the son'.

John (the Baptist)

Jesus' cousin on his mother's side, born a few months before Jesus; his father was a **priest**. He acted as a prophet, baptizing in the Jordan – dramatically re-enacting the **Exodus** from Egypt – to prepare people, by **repentance**, for God's coming judgment. He may have had some contact with the **Essenes**, though his eventual public message was different from theirs. Jesus' own vocation was decisively confirmed at his **baptism** by John. As part of John's message of the **kingdom**, he outspokenly criticized Herod Antipas for marrying his brother's wife. Herod had him imprisoned, and then beheaded him at his wife's request (Mark 6.14–29). Groups of John's disciples continued a separate existence, without merging into Christianity, for some time afterwards (e.g. Acts 19.1–7).

justified, justification

God's declaration, from his position as judge of all the world, that someone is in the right, despite universal sin. This declaration will be made on the last day on the basis of an entire life (Romans 2.1–16), but is brought forward into the present on the basis of Jesus' achievement, because sin has been dealt with through his cross (Romans 3.21—4.25); the means of this present justification is simply **faith**. This means, particularly, that Jews and **Gentiles** alike are full members of the family promised by God to Abraham (Galatians 3; Romans 4).

kingdom of God, kingdom of heaven

Best understood as the king*ship*, or sovereign and saving rule, of Israel's God YHWH, as celebrated in several psalms (e.g. 99.1) and prophecies (e.g. Daniel 6.26f.). Because YHWH was the creator God, when he finally became king in the way he intended this would involve setting the world to rights, and particularly rescuing Israel from its enemies. 'Kingdom of God' and various equivalents (e.g. 'No king but God!') became a revolutionary slogan around the time of Jesus. Jesus' own announcement of God's kingdom redefined these expectations around his own very different plan and vocation. His invitation to people to 'enter' the kingdom was a way of summoning them to allegiance to himself and his programme, seen as the start of God's long-awaited saving reign. For Jesus, the kingdom was coming not in a single move, but in stages, of which his own public career was one, his death and **resurrection** another, and a still future consummation another. Note that 'kingdom of **heaven**' is Matthew's preferred form for the same phrase, following a regular Jewish practice of saying 'heaven' rather than 'God'. It does not refer to a place ('heaven'), but to the fact of God's becoming king in and through Jesus and his achievement. Paul speaks of Jesus, as **Messiah**, already in possession of his kingdom, waiting to hand it over finally to the father (1 Corinthians 15.23–28; cf. Ephesians 5.5).

law, *see* Torah

legal experts, lawyers, *see* Pharisees

life, soul, spirit

Ancient people held many different views about what made human beings the special creatures they are. Some, including many Jews, believed that to be complete, humans needed bodies as well as inner

170

selves. Others, including many influenced by the philosophy of Plato (fourth century BC), believed that the important part of a human was the 'soul' (Gk: *psyche*), which at death would be happily freed from its bodily prison. Confusingly for us, the same word *psyche* is often used in the New Testament within a Jewish framework where it clearly means 'life' or 'true self', without implying a body/soul dualism that devalues the body. Human inwardness of experience and understanding can also be referred to as 'spirit'. *See also* **holy spirit, resurrection**.

message, *see* **good news**

Messiah, messianic, Christ

The Hebrew word means literally 'anointed one', hence in theory either a prophet, **priest** or king. In Greek this translates as *Christos*; 'Christ' in early Christianity was a title, and only gradually became an alternative proper name for Jesus. In practice 'Messiah' is mostly restricted to the notion, which took various forms in ancient Judaism, of the coming king who would be **David**'s true heir, through whom YHWH would bring judgment to the world, and in particular would rescue Israel from pagan enemies. There was no single template of expectations. Scriptural stories and promises contributed to different ideals and movements, often focused on (a) decisive military defeat of Israel's enemies and (b) rebuilding or cleansing the **Temple**. The **Dead Sea Scrolls** speak of two 'Messiahs', one a priest and the other a king. The universal early Christian belief that Jesus was Messiah is only explicable, granted his crucifixion by the Romans (which would have been seen as a clear sign that he was not the Messiah), by their belief that God had raised him from the dead, so vindicating the implicit messianic claims of his earlier ministry.

miracles

Like some of the old prophets, notably Elijah and Elisha, Jesus performed many deeds of remarkable power, particularly healings. The **gospels** refer to these as 'deeds of power', 'signs', 'marvels' or 'paradoxes'. Our word 'miracle' tends to imply that God, normally 'outside' the closed system of the world, sometimes 'intervenes'; miracles have then frequently been denied as a matter of principle. However, in the Bible

God is always present, however strangely, and 'deeds of power' are seen as *special* acts of a *present* God rather than as *intrusive* acts of an *absent* one. Jesus' own 'mighty works' are seen particularly, following prophecy, as evidence of his messiahship (e.g. Matthew 11.2–6).

Mishnah

The main codification of Jewish law (**Torah**) by the **rabbis**, produced in about AD 200, reducing to writing the 'oral Torah' which in Jesus' day ran parallel to the 'written Torah'. The Mishnah is itself the basis of the much larger collections of traditions in the two Talmuds (roughly AD 400).

parables

From the Old Testament onwards, prophets and other teachers used various story-telling devices as vehicles for their challenge to Israel (e.g. 2 Samuel 12.1–7). Sometimes these appeared as visions with interpretations (e.g. Daniel 7). Similar techniques were used by the **rabbis**. Jesus made his own creative adaptation of these traditions, in order to break open the world-view of his contemporaries and to invite them to share his vision of God's **kingdom** instead. His stories portrayed this as something that was *happening*, not just a timeless truth, and enabled his hearers to step inside the story and make it their own. As with some Old Testament visions, some of Jesus' parables have their own interpretations (e.g. the sower, Mark 4); others are thinly disguised retellings of the prophetic story of Israel (e.g. the wicked tenants, Mark 12).

parousia

Literally, it means 'presence', as opposed to 'absence', and is sometimes used by Paul with this sense (e.g. Philippians 2.12). It was already used in the Roman world for the ceremonial arrival of, for example, the emperor at a subject city or colony. Although the ascended Lord is not 'absent' from the church, when he 'appears' (Colossians 3.4; 1 John 3.2) in his 'second coming' this will be, in effect, an 'arrival' like that of the emperor, and Paul uses it thus in 1 Corinthians 15.23; 1 Thessalonians 2.19; etc. In the **gospels** it is found only in Matthew 24 (vv. 3, 27, 39).

Pharisees, legal experts, lawyers, rabbis

The Pharisees were an unofficial but powerful Jewish pressure group through most of the first centuries BC and AD. Largely lay-led, though including some **priests**, their aim was to purify Israel through intensified observance of the Jewish law (**Torah**), developing their own traditions about the precise meaning and application of scripture, their own patterns of prayer and other devotion, and their own calculations of the national hope. Though not all legal experts were Pharisees, most Pharisees were thus legal experts.

They effected a democratization of Israel's life, since for them the study and practice of Torah was equivalent to worshipping in the **Temple** – though they were adamant in pressing their own rules for the Temple liturgy on an unwilling (and often **Sadducean**) priesthood. This enabled them to survive AD 70 and, merging into the early rabbinic movement, to develop new ways forward. Politically they stood up for ancestral traditions, and were at the forefront of various movements of revolt against both pagan overlordship and compromised Jewish leaders. By Jesus' day there were two distinct schools, the stricter one of Shammai, more inclined towards armed revolt, and the more lenient one of Hillel, ready to live and let live.

Jesus' debates with the Pharisees are at least as much a matter of agenda and policy (Jesus strongly opposed their separatist nationalism) as about details of theology and piety. Saul of Tarsus was a fervent right-wing Pharisee, presumably a Shammaite, until his conversion.

After the disastrous war of AD 66–70, these schools of Hillel and Shammai continued bitter debate on appropriate policy. Following the further disaster of AD 135 (the failed Bar-Kochba revolt against Rome) their traditions were carried on by the rabbis who, though looking to the earlier Pharisees for inspiration, developed a Torah-piety in which personal holiness and purity took the place of political agendas.

present age, age to come, eternal life

By the time of Jesus many Jewish thinkers divided history into two periods: 'the present age' and 'the age to come' – the latter being the time when YHWH would at last act decisively to judge evil, to rescue Israel, and to create a new world of justice and peace. The early Christians believed that, though the full blessings of the coming age lay still in the future, it had already begun with Jesus, particularly with his death and **resurrection**, and that by **faith** and **baptism** they were able to enter it already. 'Eternal life' does not mean simply 'existence continuing without end', but 'the life of the age to come'.

priests, high priest

Aaron, the older brother of Moses, was appointed Israel's first high priest (Exodus 28—29), and in theory his descendants were Israel's priests thereafter. Other members of his tribe (Levi) were 'Levites', performing other liturgical duties but not sacrificing. Priests lived among the people all around the country, having a local teaching role (Leviticus 10.11; Malachi 2.7), and going to Jerusalem by rotation to perform the **Temple** liturgy (e.g. Luke 2.8).

David appointed Zadok (whose Aaronic ancestry is sometimes questioned) as high priest, and his family remained thereafter the senior priests in Jerusalem, probably the ancestors of the **Sadducees**. One explanation about the **Qumran** Essenes is that they were a dissident group who believed themselves to be the rightful chief priests.

Qumran, *see* Dead Sea Scrolls

rabbis, *see* Pharisees

repentance

Literally, this means 'turning back'. It is widely used in the Old Testament and subsequent Jewish literature to indicate both a personal turning away from sin and Israel's corporate turning away from idolatry and back to YHWH. Through both meanings, it is linked to the idea of 'return from **exile**'; if Israel is to 'return' in all senses, it must 'return' to YHWH. This is at the heart of the summons of both **John the Baptist** and Jesus. In Paul's writings it is mostly used for **Gentiles** turning away from idols to serve the true God; also for sinning Christians who need to return to Jesus.

resurrection

In most biblical thought, human bodies matter and are not merely disposable prisons for the **soul**. When ancient Israelites wrestled with the goodness and justice of YHWH, the creator, they ultimately came to insist that he must raise the dead (Isaiah 26.19; Daniel 12.2–3) – a suggestion firmly resisted by classical pagan thought. The longed-for return from **exile** was also spoken of in terms of YHWH raising dry bones to new **life** (Ezekiel 37.1–14). These ideas were developed in the second-**Temple** period, not least at times of martyrdom (e.g. 2 Maccabees 7). Resurrection was not just 'life after death', but a newly embodied life *after* 'life after death'; those at present dead were either 'asleep', or seen as 'souls', 'angels' or 'spirits', awaiting new embodiment.

The early Christian belief that Jesus had been raised from the dead was not that he had 'gone to **heaven**', or that he had been 'exalted', or was 'divine'; they believed all those as well, but each could have been expressed without mention of resurrection. Only the bodily resurrection of Jesus explains the rise of the early church, particularly its belief in Jesus' messiahship (which his crucifixion would have called into question). The early Christians believed that they themselves would be raised to a new, transformed bodily life at the time of the Lord's return or **parousia** (e.g. Philippians 3.20f.).

sabbath

The Jewish sabbath, the seventh day of the week, was a regular reminder both of creation (Genesis 2.3; Exodus 20.8–11) and of the **Exodus** (Deuteronomy 5.15). Along with **circumcision** and the food laws, it was one of the badges of Jewish identity within the pagan world of late antiquity, and a considerable body of Jewish **law** and custom grew up around its observance.

sacrifice

Like all ancient people, the Israelites offered animal and vegetable sacrifices to their God. Unlike others, they possessed a highly detailed written code (mostly in Leviticus) for what to offer and how to offer it; this in turn was developed in the **Mishnah** (*c.* AD 200). The Old Testament specifies that sacrifices can only be offered in the Jerusalem **Temple**; after this was destroyed in AD 70, sacrifices ceased, and Judaism developed further the idea, already present in some teachings, of prayer, fasting and almsgiving as alternative forms of sacrifice. The early Christians used the language of sacrifice in connection with such things as holiness, evangelism and the **eucharist**.

Sadducees

By Jesus' day, the Sadducees were the aristocracy of Judaism, possibly tracing their origins to the family of Zadok, **David**'s **high priest**. Based in Jerusalem, and including most of the leading priestly families, they had their own traditions and attempted to resist the pressure of the **Pharisees** to conform to theirs. They claimed to rely only on the Pentateuch (the first five books of the Old Testament), and denied any doctrine of a future life, particularly of the **resurrection** and other ideas associated with it, presumably because of the encouragement such beliefs gave to revolutionary movements. No writings from the Sadducees have survived, unless the apocryphal book of Ben Sirach ('Ecclesiasticus') comes from them. The Sadducees themselves did not survive the destruction of Jerusalem and the **Temple** in AD 70.

the satan, 'the accuser', demons

The Bible is never very precise about the identity of the figure known as 'the satan'. The Hebrew word means 'the accuser', and at times the satan seems to be a member of YHWH's heavenly council, with special responsibility as director of prosecutions (1 Chronicles 21.1; Job 1—2; Zechariah 3.1f.). However, it becomes identified variously with the serpent of the garden of Eden (Genesis 3.1–15) and with the rebellious daystar cast out of **heaven** (Isaiah 14.12–15), and was seen by many Jews as the quasi-personal source of evil standing behind both human wickedness and large-scale injustice, sometimes operating through semi-independent 'demons'. By Jesus' time various words were used to denote this figure, including Beelzebul/b (lit. 'Lord of the flies') and simply 'the evil one'; Jesus warned his followers against the deceits this figure could perpetrate. His opponents accused him of being in league with the satan, but the early Christians believed that Jesus in fact defeated it both in his own struggles with temptation (Matthew 4; Luke 4), his exorcisms of demons, and his death (1 Corinthians 2.8; Colossians 2.15). Final victory over this ultimate enemy is thus assured (Revelation 20), though the struggle can still be fierce for Christians (Ephesians 6.10–20).

scribes

In a world where many could not write, or not very well, a trained class of writers ('scribes') performed the important function of drawing up contracts for business, marriage, etc. Many would thus be legal experts, and quite possibly **Pharisees**, though being a scribe was compatible with various political and religious standpoints. The work of Christian scribes was of vital importance in copying early Christian writings, particularly the stories about Jesus.

son of David, David's son

An alternative, and infrequently used, title for **Messiah**. The messianic promises of the Old Testament often focus specifically on David's son, for example 2 Samuel 7.12–16; Psalm 89.19–37. Joseph, Mary's husband, is called 'son of David' by the angel in Matthew 1.20.

son of God

Originally a title for Israel (Exodus 4.22) and the Davidic king (Psalm 2.7); also used of ancient angelic figures (Genesis 6.2). By the New Testament period it was already used as a **messianic** title, for example in the **Dead Sea Scrolls**. There, and when used of Jesus in the **gospels** (e.g. Matthew 16.16), it means, or reinforces, 'Messiah', without the later significance of 'divine'. However, already in Paul the transition to the fuller meaning (one who was already equal with God and was sent by him to become human and to become Messiah) is apparent, without loss of the meaning 'Messiah' itself (e.g. Galatians 4.4).

soul, *see* life

spirit, *see* life, holy spirit

Temple

The Temple in Jerusalem was planned by **David** (*c.* 1000 BC) and built by his son Solomon as the central sanctuary for all Israel. After reforms under Hezekiah and Josiah in the seventh century BC, it was destroyed by Babylon in 587 BC. Rebuilding by the returned **exiles** began in 538 BC, and was completed in 516, initiating the 'second Temple period'. Judas Maccabaeus cleansed it in 164 BC after its desecration by Antiochus

Epiphanes (167). Herod the Great began to rebuild and beautify it in 19 BC; the work was completed in AD 63. The Temple was destroyed by the Romans in AD 70. Many Jews believed it should and would be rebuilt; some still do. The Temple was not only the place of **sacrifice**; it was believed to be the unique dwelling of YHWH on earth, the place where **heaven** and earth met.

Torah, Jewish law

'Torah', narrowly conceived, consists of the first five books of the Old Testament, the 'five books of Moses' or 'Pentateuch'. (These contain much law, but also much narrative.) It can also be used for the whole Old Testament scriptures, though strictly these are the 'law, prophets and writings'. In a broader sense, it refers to the whole developing corpus of Jewish legal tradition, written and oral; the oral Torah was initially codified in the **Mishnah** around AD 200, with wider developments found in the two Talmuds, of Babylon and Jerusalem, codified around AD 400. Many Jews in the time of Jesus and Paul regarded the Torah as being so strongly God-given as to be almost itself, in some sense, divine; some (e.g. Ben Sirach 24) identified it with the figure of 'Wisdom'. Doing what Torah said was not seen as a means of earning God's favour, but rather of expressing gratitude, and as a key badge of Jewish identity.

word, *see* **good news**

YHWH

The ancient Israelite name for God, from at least the time of the **Exodus** (Exodus 6.2f.). It may originally have been pronounced 'Yahweh', but by the time of Jesus it was considered too holy to speak out loud, except by the **high priest** once a year in the Holy of Holies in the **Temple**. Instead, when reading scripture, pious Jews would say *Adonai*, 'Lord', marking this usage by adding the vowels of *Adonai* to the consonants of YHWH, eventually producing the hybrid 'Jehovah'. The word YHWH is formed from the verb 'to be', combining 'I am who I am', 'I will be who I will be', and perhaps 'I am because I am', emphasizing YHWH's sovereign creative power.